GHOST STORIES
of the OLD WEST

Dan Asfar

Lone Pine Publishing International

Distributed by Lone Pine Publishing
1808-B Street NW, Suite 140
Auburn, WA
USA 98001

Website: http://www.lonepinepublishing.com

National Library of Canada Cataloguing in Publication Data

Asfar, Dan, 1973–
     Ghost stories of the Old West / Dan Asfar.
     ISBN 13: 978-1-894877-17-6
     ISBN 10: 1-894877-17-9
     1. Ghosts—West (U.S.) 2. Legends—West (U.S.) I. Title.
GR109.A83 2003   398.2'097805   C2003-910276-9

Photo Credits: Every effort has been made to accurately credit photographers. Any errors or omissions should be directed to the publisher for changes in future editions. The photographs in this book are reproduced with the kind permission of the following sources: Arizona Historical Society (pp. 4–5, 10, 41); Bullock Hotel (pp. 139, 140); Daniel Ter-Nedden/Ghosttowngallery.com (p. 23); *The American West in the Nineteenth Century,* by John Grafton, Dover Publications, 1992 (pp. 56, 79, 85, 149, 161); Glenbow Archives, Calgary, Canada (p. 159: NA-3232-54; p. 31: NA-3050-1; p. 59: NA-2483-5; p. 63: NA-1700-5; pp. 185, 189: NA-1263-35); Institute of Texan Cultures (p. 113: L-1228-E); Library of Congress (p. 43: HABS, ARIZ,2-TOMB,18-1; p. 75: USZ62-126135; p. 101, 114: USZ62-87798; p. 120: pan 6a13787; pp. 118,131; p. 132: HABS, CAL,26-BODI,3-5; p. 149: HABS,NM,4-CIM,7-4; p. 162: HABS, KANS,101-HAN.V, 1-5; p. 165: HABS, KANS,101-HAN.V,1-9; p. 170: HABS, CAL,37-OAK,1-5; p. 198: USZ62-118650; p. 201: USZ62-118054); National Archives of Canada (p. 12: C-044200; p. 28: PA-020339; p. 209: C-038620).

The stories, folklore and legends in this book are based on the author's collection of sources including individuals whose experiences have led them to believe they have encountered phenomena of some kind or another. They are meant to entertain, and neither the publisher nor the author claims these stories represent fact.

PC: P5

For Dee-Lo,
Whose absence will haunt us all.

CONTENTS

Chapter 3: Forts

Chapter 4: Inns, Houses, Hotels

Chapter 5: Go West, Young Man

Chapter 6: Working Men

Acknowledgments

Like a deck of cards without the aces, or Yul Brynner without Steve McQueen, if not for the effort and interest of several talented and enthusiastic individuals, the book you now hold in your hands would not be what it is.

I would like to thank Alana Bevan for getting to the bottom of the wheres, whats, whens and hows of so many of the stories in this book; her research was helpful and appreciated. Thanks as well go to editors Chris Wangler, Nancy Foulds and Shelagh Kubish, whose editing know-how and sense of humor have been both a relief and a hoot, respectively.

Thanks to the people whose supernatural experiences are featured in this book. Namely, Jesse Torres for his account at the Yuma Territorial Prison; Norm Stevens and Diane for sharing their experiences in the Seth Bullock Hotel; and Bob Wilhelm, Director of the Fort Hays Museum, for his valuable information regarding the legend of Elizabeth Polly. As well, I'd like to thank Angel Brant and Karen Carter for informing me of their paranormal encounters in Tombstone, Arizona.

Finally, it would be remiss of me to neglect mentioning the other works out there that have provided leads and inspired some of the stories in this volume. Jo-Anne Christensen's *Ghost Stories of Saskatchewan* was as entertaining as it was educational. Earl Murray's seminal *Ghosts of the Old West* served as a valuable reference point for the tale of the Snake People. *Ghosts on the Range* by Debra D. Munn provided an excellent sample of some of the supernatural occurrences going on in the state of Wyoming.

Thanks all.

Introduction

I have always been taken with the mythos of the Old West, though I'd be hard pressed to pin down what, exactly, stoked this interest. Early memories of watching the three-way draw between Clint Eastwood, Eli Wallach and Lee Van Cleef in *The Good, the Bad and the Ugly* mingle with a childhood awe of James Arness' law-enforcement techniques in *Gunsmoke*. That is not to say that my appreciation of the West was informed only by popular drama. On formative road trips across the wide-open spaces of Saskatchewan, Alberta and British Columbia, I remember looking out the backseat car window, trying to imagine herds of bison as far as the eye could see. Along the winding highways through the Rockies, I looked up at the snow-capped peaks and wondered what this land must have looked like before cars, roads and national parks—feeling, during these moments, that the memory of such a time might be nearly as valuable as the reality itself. Like I said, formative road trips.

Years have passed since then, and while many other passions and interests have come and gone, I have always been aware of riders galloping into an imagined sunset somewhere in my mind. I know I'm not the only one. America's fascination with its western frontier has been well recorded. From the dime novels of the 19th century to the earliest motion pictures, the "western" has been assured a prominent place in cultural expression.

Yet the irony here is that the real western movement, as it took place during the 19th century, was, one could say, too frenetic, too fierce and far too ambitious to leave room for much thought on the effects it was having on North American culture. While eastern inhabitants always showed interest in the events on the rough edges of their civilization, it was only after the heyday of western expansion had run its course that storytellers, academics and politicians came to realize how big the western experience had become in the cultures and histories of the United States and Canada. Only after the dust settled from the massive western cash grab did citizens of the North American democracies understand how historically monumental their rush into the West actually was.

We are all familiar with the icons from this period: the gangs of cowboys driving thousands of cattle from Texan ranches to railheads in Kansan cattle towns; the dusty lines of homesteaders' wagons stretching for miles along western trails; the Indians who resisted them; and the gamblers, the gold rushes, the guns and the goons. All of us know what is meant by the "Wild West."

To this day, there are many of us who still cannot escape the legacy of this old and violent West. Just like any other era or event loaded with the tortured drama of human passions, the movement west has left an indelible mark on the land and on the people who made it what it was, and what it is today. What I'm speaking of here, of course, are ghosts. According to many, the murder, mayhem and madness of the frontier period have not receded without leaving their mark on the paranormal landscape.

These are the ghost stories that are featured in this book. Some of them are supernatural events that have been narrated so many times over the generations that they have become ingrained in the folklore of the region. No one can say who first saw the Neches River Ghost Riders or which voyageur was the first to hear the cry of "Qu'Appelle?" while canoeing to Fort Espérance, but these phenomena have been reported so much over the years that any book on ghosts of the Old West would not be complete without mentioning them. Other stories are of less frequently reported ghostly incidents, as told by people who have experienced them in the saloons, hotels, theaters and countryside of the one-time American frontier. Either way, all these tales are based on historical events particular to the lands west of the 100th meridian, all, to the best of my knowledge, finding roots in actual events, relegating the imagination of the author to a humble back seat.

In this case, I wouldn't have it any other way, for as you will quickly see, the legends of the Old West, and the denizens that populate them, are more than able to carry their own stories. Sometimes life—and afterlife—is stranger than fiction.

1

Boomtowns and Gold Rushes

The Inn at Mile 108

One of the conceits Canadians have long held over Americans is the relative lack of violence on their western frontier compared to the lawless bedlam that occurred south of the 49th parallel. While the Canadian West had the North-West Mounted Police and civilized British sensibilities, the western territories of the United States were feral lands where rampant opportunism was checked only by frequent outbursts of lethal violence. In Canada, the queen's laws were borne out on the backs of honest and able Mounties, whereas in the United States, each man carried his own law holstered on his hip. Or this story is what many Canadians would like to think.

However, as any historian of the Canadian West would attest, there was no shortage of death and difficulty on the British side of the border. While Indians in the United States were being killed off by a vengeful American army, their brethren in Canada were slowly being starved to death on treaty reservations. If carefully planned settlements like Lord Selkirk's colony on Manitoba's Red River differed greatly from the chaos of cattle towns like Dodge and Abilene, no one could say Selkirk's subjects didn't suffer their fair share of tribulation—dealing with hostile Métis, Cree and an unforgiving landscape that regularly dashed any hope for agriculture. And while there can be no denying the madness of American mining towns, the gold rush into British Columbia's Fraser River and Cariboo region was hardly a gentle affair.

True, tough government men such as Vancouver Island Governor James Douglas and the famous judge of British Columbia, Matthew Baillie Begbie, managed to stamp some semblance of order on the mad rush of gold prospectors into

The Inn at Mile 108 on the Cariboo Trail welcomed miners with good food, whiskey and the company of women.

the region. Nevertheless, a virulent element of lawlessness existed in British Columbia's gold rush—a hard and homicidal streak that was just as ugly as anything in the 1849 California Gold Rush or the 1876 stampede into South Dakota's Black Hills. In fact, of the thick book of atrocities and depravities that men visited on each other in mining camps across the West, the very worst may have occurred in Canada…in a simple roadhouse right on the Cariboo Road.

Built near the headwaters of the San Jose River, the Inn at Mile 108 on the Cariboo Trail was a welcoming wooden structure that stood three stories high, offering worn-out miners easeful respite from their work. The hotel was open for over 10 years, during which time not a day passed without the smell of Agnes McVee's lamb stew drifting down the road, luring anyone in the vicinity into the big building. But all wasn't as it seemed at Mile 108. Actually, things were downright rotten.

Agnes McVee and her husband, Jim, ran the inn, assisted by their son-in-law, a big, taciturn man named Al Riley. Agnes was the obvious leader of the three. She was a voluptuous woman, tall and broad, who bellowed her welcome to customers in a thick Scottish brogue. Legend has it that every man who set eyes on her was at the same time stricken by her unusual beauty and amazed by her incredible strength. She was able to flash a dazzling smile while hoisting a huge cauldron of stew from the kitchen. "C'mon on in, boys," she'd sing out to visitors, "stew just came off the fire."

Of course, men wouldn't come to the inn just for the stew. Agnes also served up other frontier amenities, providing several different brands of rotgut whiskey, flea-infested beds and the company of women. Business did as well as could be expected in such an isolated location. Miners came and went, but Agnes, Al, Jim and the soiled doves they employed were not getting rich. Until, that is, Agnes came up with another way to do business.

Henry Dawson was steering his wagon up to the Inn at Mile 108 early one morning in March 1875. He was widely known as one of the wealthiest miners in the region, having worked his claim alone for nearly a decade, painstakingly putting away every nugget that he dug up until he had amassed a small fortune in mineral wealth. He carried his gold around with him wherever he went, and it is estimated that he had over $11,000 worth of it in his wagon when he pulled up to the McVee inn. Agnes McVee was waiting for him at the doorway. "Well then, Mr. Dawson!" she cried out, flashing the solitary miner one of her brilliant grins. "What a pleasant surprise!"

Dawson was a man of few words and only tipped his hat as he walked into the inn. He ate in complete silence, addressing Mrs. McVee only after he had finished with his stew. "Agnes," the gruff old miner finally said, "I've a business proposition for ye."

"Business proposition?"

"Yeah, business," the miner responded, wincing as he took a swig of whiskey. "I reckon you know I've made good o'r the last few years."

"I've heard you've done alright," Agnes responded.

"Well, I'm thinkin' about making a home on my claim—a *real* home. I guess what I'm sayin' is that I'll be needin' myself a woman."

Agnes looked at the man, trying her best to look shocked. "What are you proposing Mr. Dawson?"

The miner was silent for a long moment before he answered. "Well, I was thinkin' maybe I could buy one of your girls off you."

"For good?" Agnes replied. "I mean, buy her for life…that's what yer talkin' about?"

Dawson looked Agnes straight in the eye. "Yeah, that's what I'm talkin' about. I'll offer you $2000 in gold."

Agnes was suddenly receptive. "$2000. You have that in yer wagon right now?"

"That and more," the miner said, a proud look in his eye.

"Well," Agnes replied, "you may have yourself a deal, Mr. Dawson. Why don't you stay the night while me and Jim have a talk about this?"

If the unfortunate practice of buying brides wasn't uncommon in the Old West, neither was it so ordinary that it didn't warrant commemoration by the buyers. Henry Dawson, deciding that he had cause for celebration, called out to Jim McVee for another shot of whiskey, followed by another and another yet. Meanwhile, Agnes sneaked out the back door, to where Al Riley waited in the bushes with a rifle in his hands. "Now's the time," she hissed at her son-in-law. "He's getting soused in the front room."

Al crept around the inn to the front window, rested his rifle on the sill, aimed carefully and fired, blowing a hole through Henry Dawson's back, killing him instantly. Agnes and Al wasted no time. Hauling the dead miner's body out of the inn, they carried him back to his wagon, where Jim was already unloading Dawson's gold. After they had removed every nugget and the last whiff of gold dust, Jim McVee then drove the wagon several miles from the inn, unhitched his horse and pushed it into a lake just off the Cariboo Road. When the authorities found the wagon with Dawson's body in it, they concluded that he must have been robbed and killed while traveling on the wagon road.

As for Agnes, Jim and Al, their success inspired them to continue their nefarious operation. They killed only patrons who were at the inn when no one else was there, usually disposing of them the same way they killed Dawson. It didn't matter who it was, the three murdered without discrimination. Merchants, gold miners, bordello madams and alpine farmers all became victims at Mile 108. Pretty well every man that came up to Mile 108 to buy one of Agnes' girls got himself a bullet in the back. The countryside became a virtual graveyard over the next several years; one by one, dead bodies kept turning up, until the corpse count was numbered at over 59. Oddly enough, the local authorities never suspected the proprietors of the Inn at Mile 108. Convinced that a group of homicidal highwaymen were at work, the law turned its attention to the surrounding wilderness, but no matter how thoroughly posses combed the forests, no trace of a band of robbers was ever found.

Who knows how long this murderous operation would have continued if a young gambler by the name of MacDonald hadn't shown up at the inn in the spring of 1884? He was a drifter and a gambler returning home to Montana after spending a few years plying his dubious trade in Barkerville. His saddlebags were near bursting with his ill-gotten lucre, and he wanted only one more thing from the Cariboo before he went back to Montana—a wife. He arrived at the Inn at Mile 108 in the early evening, the only patron in the building that night. Al Riley greeted him, serving up a bowl of the house stew and a few glasses of whiskey while Jim McVee loaded his rifle in the back of the inn. MacDonald would have met his end within the hour if Agnes hadn't walked into the dining room when she did.

For when the matriarch looked at the solitary young man wolfing down her lamb stew, she fell instantly and completely in love. She rushed up to Al Riley, who was watching his quarry from behind the bar. "Who's that?" she asked breathlessly.

"How should I know?" Riley shrugged. "Calls himself MacDonald. He's here for a woman."

Agnes walked up to where MacDonald was sitting. "Hi there," she crooned to the young man. "Al tells me you're in the market for one of my girls."

"That I am, miss," MacDonald said between mouthfuls. "I'm goin' back home to Montana, and intend to be married before I get there."

"Well, I know just the one for you," Agnes replied. "The best girl I've got, and all it'll cost you is $4000 in gold." Before she went up to get the girl, Agnes walked into the kitchen and told her husband to put the rifle down. "We're calling this one off," she said. "This man's gonna get the bride he paid for."

Returning from the second floor with a young woman in tow, Agnes handed her over to MacDonald in exchange for a bag of gold nuggets. She stood back to appraise the sight of the young couple standing in front of her. "Lord, what a handsome pair ye make," she beamed. "Now make sure you head straight for a preacher and do this proper-like."

MacDonald spent the night at the inn, and the next morning Agnes, Jim and Al were standing at the doorway as the couple rode off down the Cariboo Road. Agnes McVee waved at them. "Look at that," she sighed to Al Riley and her husband. "There's nothing in the world like the sight of a young couple in love." Neither of the men joined her when she burst out in raucous laughter. Indeed, if Agnes bothered to look, she might have been concerned by the ugly scowl smeared across her husband's face.

Jim McVee was none too happy that they let MacDonald get away just because Agnes took a fancy to him, and while Jim was able to swallow his pride as the freshly acquainted pair rode away from the inn, by midday he decided that he would never be able to respect himself if MacDonald got away. Loading up his horse, Jim hit the Cariboo Road after dinner, telling Agnes and Al that he was off for a short leisure trip.

He didn't return until well past midnight, leading a riderless pinto by the reins. Agnes and Al were sitting in their empty bar, throwing back glasses of whiskey, when the clatter of horse hooves in the stables announced his arrival. "That'll be my fool husband," Agnes said. "Why don't you go see what's taken him so long?"

Al was back before long, standing uncomfortably in front of Agnes McVee. "Jim's got that MacDonald boy's horse with him," Al said, avoiding Agnes' gaze. "He's got bags of gold too."

It was as if Agnes wasn't allowing herself to understand. "How can that be?" she asked her son-in-law.

"Jim killed him, Agnes. The boy is dead."

Without saying a word, the dame of Mile 108 got up from where she sat, walked up to her room and quietly shut the door behind her. The next morning, both Jim and Al were surprised to find Agnes already up, cheerfully stirring a pot of porridge in the kitchen. Singing to herself as she put the two steaming bowls in front of Al and Jim, Agnes tussled her husband's hair playfully and sat down next to him with her own bowl of breakfast.

Agnes had a way of brightening up a room when she was in the right mood, and that morning, the inn was glowing. Agnes cracked one joke after another, and the room was full of laughter. Until, that is, Jim began to choke. Coughing and wheezing, he tumbled from his stool, writhing on the floor as foam bubbled through his lips. "You've poisoned him," a shocked Al Riley said to the woman sitting across from him.

But Agnes did nothing to acknowledge her wheezing husband. She kept up her casual banter until Jim stopped breathing. Then her tone changed. She was suddenly serious. "Let's bury this fool in the back."

The couple had just picked up Jim's dead body when the law burst through the front door of the inn. Both Agnes McVee and Al Riley were arrested on the spot. It turned out that while Jim had indeed killed MacDonald the night before, his newly purchased bride managed to get away. She went straight to the local sheriff after she was freed and told them everything about the Inn at Mile 108.

During the upcoming months, Agnes and Al denied everything, but the evidence against them was overwhelming. The shocked authorities found eight girls imprisoned in the inn, scared witless and half starved. They were so terrified of Agnes that none of them would say anything about their experiences at the roadhouse, but the remnants of death all around the inn spoke volumes. Investigators found charred bones in the hotel's fireplaces; dozens of buried corpses were unearthed around the building. By the summer of 1885, there was more than enough evidence against Agnes and Al to put them on the gallows. Yet Agnes was unwilling to subject herself to a public trial. Swallowing a vial of poison she had sneaked into prison, she took her own life the night before she was to go to court. Al's trial was a swift affair; found guilty of multiple charges of kidnapping and murder, he was promptly hanged for his role in the killings.

Years passed and the evil proprietors of the Inn at Mile 108 passed into local legend. In 1892, the original building was torn down and rebuilt on the other side of the Cariboo Road; a post house, store and telegraph station were attached. The gold rush subsided; new settlers came with the intention of making crops grow from soil; old adventurers left for new opportunities. The years passed and the horror of the atrocities faded, but they would never be completely forgotten.

People were always conscious that most of the gold the trio stole was never found. In 1924, a local farmer found $2500 in gold buried on his property. Years later, a second cache of gold nuggets was unearthed, this one worth over $6000. There's nothing like the idea of buried treasure to keep a legend alive, and the estimated $100,000 of unclaimed gold buried around Mile 108 has ensured that the legend remains. But it is not just the allure of buried treasure that kept the morbid tale of Mile 108 circulating. For strange things began to be reported around the area soon after Al Riley was hanged.

It started with the lights. Travelers who found themselves around Mile 108 during the gloaming hours saw them—orbs of light that bobbed up and flashed in the not-too-distant darkness. Some saw white lights, others said yellow and still others claimed they were red. Regardless of color, everyone who laid eyes on them felt the same sense of foreboding, struck by an unpleasant certainty that whatever they were, they weren't friendly. More than one frazzled traveler intending to set up camp kept riding through the night to put as much distance as possible between themselves and the ominous light show.

Those who bore witness to the lights at Mile 108 never had anything good to say about the experience, but some travelers had much more unpleasant encounters near the McVees' old inn. People setting up camp in the area would be woken in the middle of the night by horrible screams and blood-chilling laughter coming from the darkness. According to witnesses, there was nothing subtle or remote about these sounds—they were loud and terrible, seeming to come from the mouths of terrible beings that were just beyond their firelight. Travelers who didn't immediately pack up and hit the road right then and there would be kept up the entire night by these unearthly sounds waxing and waning throughout the night.

And then there were the stories of travelers who slept through the night without being disturbed, only to wake up and find that their mounts had been taken in the night. Horses and mules vanished without a trace, leaving not even the slightest tracks to mark their passing; indeed, these animals' disappearances were so complete that no one suspected bandits were responsible. The mysterious animal thefts were quickly linked to the other bizarre occurrences around Mile 108, and it was deemed these vanishing acts were the work of the many discontented and vengeful spirits that fell victim to the McVees' machinations.

The strange happenings along that stretch of the Cariboo Road continued to get stranger. By the late 1880s, the legend of the road took on a life of its own, and word began spreading that men were disappearing around Mile 108 again. Then it stopped. When the McVee roadhouse was torn down in 1892, no one heard another story about flashing lights, strange sounds or vanishing animals. The hills around Mile

108 went suddenly silent and dark at night; no more animals went missing inexplicably, and people began stopping at Mile 108 again. The brutal McVee killings and the haunting of the area passed into legend. And while no one would ever be able to explain the shadow that fell over the region between 1885 and 1892, it was largely suspected that Agnes, Jim and Al were still responsible—somehow reaching beyond the grave to continue their reign of death and misery over the region that was once theirs.

The Ghosts of Dawson

What used to be the town of Dawson lies in the Sangre de Cristo Mountains in Colfax County, New Mexico, some 15 miles northeast of the town of Cimarron. There isn't much left of the once-bustling mining community. Accessible by a single dirt road branching off Highway 64, Dawson is in the middle of a dusty nowhere, overrun by sagebrush and rattlesnakes. The only indications that the town ever stood are a commemorative placard situated on the abandoned town site and the Dawson Cemetery, a burial ground still marked by an old iron fence. The placard is a state historical marker, telling an abridged version of the ghost town's short history, while the Dawson Cemetery is a plot of earth riddled with far too many identical white crosses, which, many would say, whisper a story all their own.

Unlike so many mining towns before it that sprang up around mineral wealth, Dawson was distinctly modern in that it was planned and financed by a single corporation. The site was purchased in 1867 by a rancher named J.B. Dawson,

The Dawson Cemetery is haunted with the souls of hundreds of miners—men who lost their lives in mining disasters.

who operated a ranch there until 1901, when the Dawson Fuel Company purchased the 20,000 acres with the intention of capitalizing on an enormous coal seam that had been discovered on a nearby mountain. But it wasn't until 1903, when Phelps Dodge bought the land, that the town of Dawson was born.

At its peak, Dawson boasted nearly 9000 residents. The Phelps Dodge Company oversaw the construction of homes for its workers and their families. There were fully staffed hospitals. For children, there were schools; for culture, an opera house; and for entertainment, a bowling alley. At its peak, Dawson was a shining example of what a mining community could be. A far cry from the Leadvilles, Deadwoods and Sacramentos of the world, Dawson marked the end of the murderous madness that accompanied most mining towns of the American West. Nevertheless, when death came to Dawson, it came on a scale that put every other violent frontier town to shame.

Disaster struck on October 22, 1913. A faulty dynamite charge blew the insides out of one of the mines, killing almost everyone inside. By the time all the bodies were accounted for, it was determined that 263 men had perished in the explosion. It was one of the worst mining disasters in American history. The victims were buried in a special part of the Dawson Cemetery, their anonymous graves marked with small iron crosses.

From then on, Dawson's graveyard loomed larger in the public consciousness than the town itself. Whatever the people of Dawson were doing day to day, no one could ignore the sprawling stretch of corpses on the side of the mountain. No Boot Hill in any western town could compete with the air of death and desolation that hung over the town cemetery. The graveyard eventually seemed to take on a life of its own, and no one in Dawson was ever the same because of it. Soon after the disaster, frightening stories began to spread through the town. Some heard strange sounds—unlike anything produced by cricket or coyote—drifting down from the graveyard, long lingering wails or moans that would come and go throughout the night. Others passing by the cemetery gates after sunset claimed to see dim humanoid shapes walking through the darkness, vague forms that vanished the moment anyone tried to take a closer look.

Citizens of Dawson quickly decided that their cemetery was haunted. Locals assumed that the graveyard was full of miners' spirits that were angry or confused at their sudden and needless deaths. Looking back, however, it might be said that the ghosts of Dawson Cemetery were trying to warn the living. For on February 8, 1923, 10 years after the first mining accident broke Dawson's heart, another explosion tore through a crowded mine. And another 123 miners gave up their lives digging for coal.

The men's remains were dug out of the rubble and buried alongside the bodies from the 1913 disaster, identical small iron crosses marking the graves of the nameless dead. So it was that two of the worst mining disasters in the United States' history took place in a humble New Mexico town. The Dawson Cemetery, now bristling with 386 miners' crosses, became a monument to Dawson's darker side. After 1923, whatever went on within the town itself was overshadowed by the specter of death that hung over the graveyard.

It's fitting, then, that curiosity seekers looking for the mining town in northern New Mexico today will find only desolate Dawson Cemetery. While the rest of the original buildings in town are either torn down or now located on private property, the cemetery is open to anyone who cares to see it. The iron gate to the burial ground still stands under the blazing southwestern sun, its metal letters, spelling "DAWSON," somehow ominous on the lonely mountain. And unlike the residents of the mining town, who left the borough shortly after Phelps Dodge shut down the mines in 1950, the ghosts of the Dawson Cemetery have remained behind.

There are countless stories of strange happenings in the graveyard. Daytime visitors often claim to have heard barely audible whispers on the wind, the voices of men warning of some unseen and unfathomable danger. Others speak of fierce cold spots that surround specific gravesites: people who were sweating a few moments before find themselves shivering in the sudden chill. The cold spell lasts for a few short moments before lifting without warning, leaving witnesses frightened and confused, wondering what, exactly, they had just experienced.

But the most dramatic accounts of ghosts in the Dawson Cemetery are set during the evening hours. That is when the daytime whispers become full-throated moans drifting over the burial ground. Curiosity seekers and investigators have witnessed balls of light floating over the expanse of iron crosses. Some claim to have spotted vaguely human-shaped patches of glowing fog drifting through the graveyard. The forms hover for a few moments before dissipating into the night air, leaving no trace that they were ever there.

It might be more suitable to call the dead of Dawson Cemetery corporate casualties rather than men who were felled by the violence of the Old West. They were, after all, employees of Phelps Dodge—men who were taken care of by the company that settled them, men who never had to worry about gunfighters, cowboys or Indians. Yet the miners who died in Dawson were subjected to a sort of violence that could only be called western. Like cowboys, teamsters, lawmen and outlaws, the miners of Dawson risked their lives to make a buck, and in the end, for 386 of them, their rough jobs on the hard periphery of the United States cost them their lives. They still don't seem too happy about it.

Dead Man in Barkerville

Like a rose in a briar or a bride in a bordello, Wellington Delaney Moses stood out amongst the rough rabble of frontier America. A man who invariably chose silk over denim, wine over whiskey and soap instead of spit, Moses strutted through the dust and dirt of the West's worst boomtowns with an unmistakable—if improbable—air of gentility. In a world where manners could easily be mistaken for weakness, and weakness might get you killed, Moses' ostentatious displays of refinement made him a virtual alien. And as if his carefully pomaded hair and gold watch fob weren't enough, Moses was also a black man. "Well look here," boorish San Franciscans would jeer as Moses walked down a planked sidewalk, shining head held high, "these scallywags are still slaves out east, and this man's strutting around like a goddamn prince."

Moses was never fazed by this kind of talk. In fact, he thrived on it. For while it was true that in the 1850s, most black Americans were tied to southern plantations in the Old South, Moses wasn't too concerned with the issue of slavery. Because like everyone else who was out West, Moses was there to make a buck, and for the line of work he was in, public attention equaled greenbacks. This western jim-dandy ran a barbershop and bathhouse in San Francisco during its early years. While he was known as one of the best in his profession, he made most of his money hawking his famous

If Wellington Moses hadn't met James Barry at 70 Mile House (above), he might never have encountered the blood-chilling sight that he did.

"Hair Invigorator," a cosmetic panacea that, when applied to the scalp, would restore lost hair, give a coiffure a shining gloss and cure headaches to boot. Moses himself was a walking advertisement for his product, claiming that his own full head of hair was once bare as a cue ball. "But that was before I started using Hair Invigorator," Moses would say to soon-to-be buyers. "I got the recipe from an old Indian Medicine Man. I challenge you, my friends: point out *one* bald Indian."

Moses made a good living selling his snake oil to unwitting San Franciscans for a short while. Yet the nature of his business wouldn't allow him to stay in the bustling gold town for too long. Dissatisfied customers accumulated daily, and it wasn't long before a good number of westerners, bald and angry, wanted to do him harm. Not the kind of man to outstay a welcome, Moses left San Francisco in 1858, taking a ship up to Victoria, on Vancouver Island, where he promptly set up another shop.

But business in this colonial town wasn't nearly as brisk as it was further south. For some reason, Moses found that it was more difficult to convince British subjects of his Hair Invigorator's efficacy. Quickly deciding that he needed a more ingenuous market, Moses turned his attention to rougher frontier towns. Luckily for him, the Cariboo Gold Rush was just about to sweep through the interior of British Columbia.

Some time in 1865, Moses packed up his razor, his strop and a few crates of Hair Invigorator and headed up the Cariboo Road, planning on setting up in Barkerville, the most far-flung town on the Cariboo Trail. Beginning his journey in the town of Yale, Moses met and befriended a career adventurer named Charles Morgan Blessing, who was heading up to Barkerville as well. The two men traveled the road north together and quickly became fast friends. Blessing told Moses tales of his travels through the West, and Moses, for his part, abstained from trying to sell Blessing any of his wares.

Their relationship changed when they arrived at Cariboo Trail's 70 Mile House; it was there, while they were throwing back a few shots of overpriced whiskey in the over-crowded roadhouse, that they met James Barry. Barry was a Texan gambler on his way up to Barkerville as well, hoping to cash in on the mining town's lively gaming scene. Accompanying Moses and Blessing for the rest of the way to Barkerville, Barry quickly made the northern journey into an intolerable affair. If the Texan was civil enough when he met the pair, his onerous nature began to emerge almost as soon as the trio set foot outside 70 Mile House.

Any man spending time in western mining towns would have been well acquainted with boorishness, but the vehement bitterness of James Barry was enough to get through even the thickest skin. If Moses and Blessing were able to deal with the Texan's near constant diatribes against anything and everything in the wide world, his vehement and voluble racism took its toll on Moses and Blessing's friendship. By the time the trio reached Williams Lake, Moses was ready to go his own way.

He split up with Blessing and Barry in the town of Quesnel, staying behind for a few days to provide the miners there with some badly needed shaves and haircuts, as well as a few bottles of his hair tonic. Moses made the last leg of the journey to Barkerville alone and promptly set up another barbershop when he got there. Business was good.

So good, in fact, that he had little time or opportunity to check up on Charles Blessing. He finally did run into a drunk Jim Barry in one of the town's saloons. Barry was none too friendly, making it known as loudly as possible that no man of color was any friend of his. When Moses asked about Blessing, however, Barry went oddly quiet. "I've got no idea what became of that yellow belly," he said. "I guess he just lost the stomach for the life. Halfway between here and Quesnel, he up and left—just turned around and went back the other way. Didn't say a word as to why."

Wellington Moses spent the rest of his life in Barkerville, running his bar-bershop, and often told the tale of when he shaved a dead man.

Moses trusted Barry about as much as he liked him and didn't put too much stock in the drunken blowhard's story, but in the Old West, there was a word for men who asked too many questions: dead. So Moses went back to business, doing his best to shut Blessing and Barry from his mind.

Who knows? He might have succeeded in putting the past behind him, if forces bigger than Wellington Delaney Moses did not have other plans. The nightmare began exactly one week after Moses spoke to Barry. Moses was cleaning up shop after the last customer of the day when the bell on the door rang. "Sorry partner," Moses said without looking up from his sweeping. "I'm closed up for the day; come back tomorrow."

Whoever was at the door was silent, but the sound of heels on the floor made it evident that he hadn't heard Moses; the barber got irritated. "Listen man, I said I'm…" Moses was unable to finish his sentence, so dumbstruck was he by the sight in front of him. Standing there in his barbershop was none other than Charles Morgan Blessing. "Jesus, Charlie," Moses gasped, unable to contain his shock, "what in tarnation happened? You look half dead!"

Moses wasn't exaggerating; his friend's face was the color of faded paper and his eyes were strangely blank, disturbingly lifeless. There was a moment of silence, while Charlie just stood there, staring straight through Wellington Moses. "Well, then," Moses said, suddenly uncomfortable, "what can I do for you?" Charlie sat down on the barber's chair without saying a word. "Well, you do need a shave right badly. This shouldn't take a second."

Moses threw a hot towel over Blessing's face and turned to get his straight razor. The sight that greeted him when he looked back at Blessing's covered head made him swoon with horror. A second ago, Moses' friend was lying back in the chair with a clean white facecloth; now the cloth was soaked in blood—red drops dripping down the sides of Blessing's face onto his clothes and the floor. The barber could only stand in shock when a deep and anguished voice came from under the facecloth. "Sarah Murphy," it said. "Talk to Sarah Murphy."

And then he was gone. Wellington let out a little shout when Blessing vanished. The terrified barber stared at where his friend had just been sitting, his eyes fixed on the blood-soaked towel on the chair, on the streaks of blood that were still dripping onto the barbershop floor. For long moments, Moses didn't know what to believe. He doubted his eyes; he doubted his sanity; he doubted reality. Yet through all of this he held onto the one thing the terrifying visitor had said: "Talk to Sarah Murphy." Besides the bloody mess, this message was all Blessing had left.

Moses knew Sarah Murphy well. She was one of the popular hurdy gurdy girls, a dancing troupe that toured the Barkerville watering holes. He had spoken to her often in the past, but now found himself hesitant at approaching her. It took Moses a couple of days, but he finally worked up the courage to approach the young woman after one of her shows. He waited until the crowd around her dispersed and then sauntered up, as casually as he could. "Hello there, Sarah, hell of a show tonight."

Sarah turned towards Moses, smiling brightly at the sight of the nattily dressed barber. "Well look at you, Wellington. It's been quite some time, hasn't it?"

Moses was about to respond, but the sight of the necklace hanging around her neck caught his tongue and froze his heart. Tied to a simple leather chord was a gold nugget shaped like a tiny human skull. Moses had seen this same nugget before, hanging around Charlie Blessing's throat; it was his most prized possession. When they were riding up to Barkerville, Charlie told the story about how he had won the nugget in a poker game from none other than the famous Mexican bandit, Joaquim Murrieta. "What is it, Moses?" Sarah asked of the stunned barber.

"Where did you get that nugget?"

"It was given to me by an admirer," Sarah responded, obviously put off by Moses' manner.

"Who?"

"Well, if you must know, it was from a Texan gentleman named James Barry."

Moses was instantly seized by the realization that Barry had killed his friend on the way into town. He turned his back on the dancing girl and stormed out of the saloon, all at once struggling with guilt, grief, anger and wonder. *He came back from the grave to give me this message*, Moses thought. For the first time in as long as he could remember, the frontier barber had a thought that was unrelated to turning a profit: *I have to set things right.*

He saddled up and headed out the next day, riding out to see Judge Cox in the town of Richfield, a few miles to the south. Moses told the judge the whole story, leaving out the part about Blessing's posthumous visit to his shop. Moses' information came just as a posse found Charlie's corpse carelessly buried behind some bushes just off the Cariboo Trail between Quesnel and Barkerville. Barry was arrested a few days later, held in Barkerville until August 1867, when the famous Cariboo Gold Rush judge, Matthew Baillie Begbie, arrived to conduct his trial. Wellington Moses was a key witness in the trial, and based largely on the information he provided, Judge Begbie ruled the Texan was guilty of murder. James Barry was hanging from his neck before the month was up.

Wellington Moses ended up spending the rest of his life in Barkerville, running his barbershop well after the rush of gold miners subsided and the mountain town settled into a modest existence. By the time he passed on in 1890, the former hairdresser and confidence man was one of the town's most loved patriarchs. He was remembered most as a man who loved to tell stories about Barkerville's wilder days. His favorite and most repeated tale began with the same phrase: "And then there was the time I almost shaved a dead man."

The Dunn Building

The town of Victor was incorporated in 1893, given life by the surge of miners that came flooding into the Cripple Creek region looking for gold. Located west of Colorado Springs, just a few miles south of the town of Cripple Creek, Victor soon came to be the economic heart of the gold mining region, surpassing Cripple Creek itself as the busiest town in the area. Like so many other mining towns across the West that mushroomed overnight, however, Victor mostly grew in unsavory directions during its formative years.

The ratio of saloons to churches in 1893 was high enough that every vagabond for miles around with an affinity for depravity and an aversion to decency might want to pay the town a visit. Surely, the badly outnumbered peace officers in town would have sworn this to be true. In 1893, the streets of Victor were crawling with every sort of bad man that there was in the West. Gamblers, gunfighters, murderers, madmen, bushwhackers, wolfers, con men and amongst these all, miners—all armed, all inebriated and all congregating in the smoky saloons that made a brisk trade off their vices. It didn't take too long for Victor's Boot Hill to become dense with pine box residents.

Indeed, Victor's morticians were almost as busy as its barkeepers, and of them all, Thomas Dunn was busiest. He practiced his trade in the Dunn Building, enjoying a rather macabre heyday during the burg's early years. His was one of the first funeral parlors in town, and by all accounts, even though he was swamped with corpses during the town's first years, Dunn was said to be the consummate professional, able to make bullet holes and mortal wounds almost disappear in the cadavers that were brought to him. Bloodied gunfighters who looked as if they might have borne some relation to wolverines or hyenas while alive came out of Dunn's funeral parlor looking like posthumous gentlemen. Miners who had come to tragic and gruesome deaths in the tunnels around town were laid to rest without any visible trace of their horrible wounds. Given that Dunn worked with the dead throughout his life, it might not come as such a surprise that strange stories about the Dunn Building abounded after the famed mortician passed away.

Paranormal enthusiasts might even say that supernatural activity could be expected, given the number of dead bodies that went in and out of the building. When Mrs. T.F. Dunn turned the building into a boarding house after Mr. Dunn passed away, there was no shortage of stories offered by boarders who stayed on the second floor of the boarding house. Residents told of sudden cold spots that would come out of nowhere, making the hair on the back of their necks stand on end. Others heard heavy footsteps slowly making their way through rooms and sometimes down the second-floor hallway, though not a man, woman or child was visible to the eye.

There were more chilling stories. Some boarders left the Dunn Building in the middle of the night, babbling hysterically about how they were awakened by a terrible suffocating feeling, as if some invisible force of incredible strength was pressing down on their lungs—only when they bolted from bed and out of their rooms were they able to breathe again. Others claimed that a pair of invisible hands, freezing and hard as stone, had wrapped themselves around their throats while they were trying to sleep, strangling the breath out of them for several terrifying moments before suddenly releasing them for no apparent reason. While no one was ever hurt physically by the spirits that haunted the Dunn Building, more than one frightened boarder would attest to their maliciousness.

For the longest time, people just assumed the spirits of those bitterly departed that once went in and out of the funeral parlor were responsible for the goings-on in the Dunn Building. Until, that is, 1899 when a man who had been one of Mr. Dunn's assistants spoke up about a disturbing incident that took place in the funeral home in 1893. His tale shed new light on the events in the old funeral parlor.

According to this man's story, it happened while Dunn was working on the corpse of a miner who had been badly mutilated in a cave-in. He had just begun preparing the miner for burial when the supposed cadaver suddenly twitched on the embalming table. A moment later, the badly bleeding corpse came to tortured life. One of its hands darted out to grab the startled mortician; the other reached up to feel the remnants of its mangled face. It was an undertaker's nightmare come true: the dead man on the table wasn't quite dead yet.

The realization hit the mortician, his assistant and the supposed-to-be-dead miner with equal force. As Dunn took a few horrified steps backward, the man on the table let out a bloodcurdling wail and tried to sit up. While the miner did manage to get up, it quickly became obvious he didn't know which way to go; he couldn't see a thing through his one remaining eye. Another frightful shriek split through the confines of the undertaker's office.

"He's delirious with pain!" Dunn yelled to his assistant through the miner's agonized wails. "Get me the morphine!"

The young man ran for the painkiller as Dunn did his best to restrain the flailing erstwhile corpse. It wasn't until they had filled the miner's veins with morphine that he finally settled down, falling in a heap on the mortuary floor. After picking the miner up and putting him back on the embalming table, Dunn's assistant turned to get help but was stopped by his employer before he was able to take a single step towards the door. "Where the hell you think you're going?" Dunn grunted at his assistant, wiping the miner's blood off his face and hands.

The assistant looked at Dunn uncomprehendingly, still shocked, uncertain of how to respond. "He isn't dead; he needs a doctor."

"Doctor!?" Dunn roared. "Look at this man. What do you think a doctor could possibly do for him?"

The young man froze in his tracks. His eyes fell on the moaning man lying on the embalming table. "What would you have me do?"

Dunn looked at his assistant for a moment before giving his response. "Get more morphine. We'll put him to rest."

Barely hesitating, Dunn's assistant did as he was told and filled another syringe with the drug. Dunn himself delivered the lethal injection and hardly waited at all before resuming his work on the miner. The young assistant couldn't help noticing that the miner was still producing a faint pulse while he was being prepared for burial.

Nevertheless, the assistant undertaker kept quiet about the affair for years, confessing the grisly deed only after the funeral parlor was turned into a boarding house and the ghost of the Dunn Building became widely known. But he didn't stop at this confession. He also told Mrs. Dunn that ever since the miner was put to death, strange things began to happen at the funeral parlor. The undertaker and his assistant became conscious of an intangible presence, malevolent and unseen, that wandered through the building. Sometimes they could hear him—his footsteps making their way across the second floor when they knew they were the only two living people in the building. On other occasions, they would feel him—his icy presence, angry and hateful, filling both of them with silent dread. As soon as Mr. Dunn died, his assistant quit the business and never once ventured back into the Dunn Building, though, it seems, the spirit of the angry miner enjoyed no such luxury.

The legend of the Dunn Building is one of those stories that refuses to die, told and retold generation after generation. To this day, psychics and paranormal investigators who have investigated the building in Victor will adamantly state that a malevolent spirit still drifts through the old building's halls, just as angry as he ever was—perhaps convinced that he may have been saved if someone put him in front of a doctor instead of a mortician so many years ago.

Tombstone

Few places west of the 100th meridian better express the American drive to make a buck like the town of Tombstone. On a sunburned stretch of Arizona dirt in the San Pedro Hills less than 20 miles from the Mexican border, Tombstone was founded in 1877 by a man named Ed Schiefflin—a foolhardy fortune hunter who stumbled upon a silver vein in a barren middle of nowhere. He named his claim "The Tombstone" to spite his detractors, who joked that the only thing he would find in the Arizona desert was his own grave. The silver strike made Schiefflin a millionaire, and thousands of prospectors hoping to emulate his success rushed into the region. So it was that the town of Tombstone practically sprung up overnight, turning the recently naked region into a beehive of activity—or maybe hornet's nest would be a better description.

The drama of Tombstone's heyday made an indelible mark on the cultural landscape of the American West. Indeed, of all the western boomtowns that took shape in the 19th century, it was Tombstone that would come to be celebrated as the embodiment of the freewheeling opportunism and violent confrontation that so often defined the Old West. There were cowboys making their living off livestock in the surrounding countryside; there were miners burrowing deep into their dark pits for silver; and there were the denizens of the town of Tombstone itself, who provided all the usual frontier amenities to the rough laborers flooding into the region.

Saloons, vaudeville houses, brothels and jailhouses. Cowboys, miners, gamblers, prostitutes, barkeepers, outlaws and lawmen. By 1898, over 10,000 people lived in this frontier

The town of Tombstone in 1881

town: thousands of individuals who came from all corners of the globe in search of the same thing—money. Some of these fortune hunters were more famous than others. As countless written pages and mile upon mile of celluloid film will attest, men such as Virgil, Morgan and Wyatt Earp, Doc Holliday and Ike Clanton are in no danger of being forgotten. Surely, the bloody vendetta between the Earps and the Clantons has shot Tombstone into legend.

But Tombstone didn't become what it was solely through the misadventures of a small group of six-gun luminaries. The town's infamous lawlessness was created one bottle of whiskey at a time, with every frustrated miner that finished a long day of grueling and fruitless labor; with every hard-earned dollar lost in one of the saloons; with every insult, real or imagined, directed at another armed young man far too jealous of his honor. Simply put, Tombstone suffered from too many men with too many guns drinking too much booze, and its reputation as one of the wildest burgs in an already too Wild West was built on the bedlam these young men made.

The Bird Cage Theatre

If Tombstone truly was the most devilish town in the West, then the Bird Cage Theatre was its belly. The notorious theater was established in 1881 and kept its doors open until 1889, when flooded mines and plummeting silver prices reduced Tombstone to a virtual ghost town. During the nine years it was open, the Bird Cage Theatre was generally acknowledged as the epicenter of madness in Tombstone. In 1882, *The New York Times* described the vaudeville house as the "wildest wickedest night spot between Basin Street and the Barbary Coast."

Every night, countless booze-soaked dramas would play themselves out in the gaslit confines of the lively theater. A soused gunslinger would glare at a long-hated rival from behind a hand of cards as his right hand slowly fell to the shooting iron at his hip. A lovesick miner would be trying his

The Bird Cage Theatre, known for wild performances in the 1880s, is now a museum, but it still has a lively afterlife.

best to convince one of the house's prostitutes that she should leave her life of sin and join him on his claim as his wife. A disbelieving man would win a small fortune in a single game of faro, while another card player a few tables over watched in despair as he lost a year of his earnings with one misplaced bet. And in the 14 curtained cribs hanging over all of this, ladies of the night plied their immoral trade. Emotions ran high in the Bird Cage Theatre, and more than one festering resentment boiled over into violence. There are over 140 bullet holes in the walls and ceiling of the theater, caused by the 16 gunfights that were said to take place there.

It might not come as such a surprise, then, that the Bird Cage Theatre is considered one of the most haunted places in town. Today, the Bird Cage is a museum, offering an immaculately preserved exhibition of Tombstone's wilder years. Many would say that it offers so much more. The first accounts of strange happenings in the theater began shortly after it was reopened to the public in 1934. Closed since the last patron threw back his last glass of whiskey in 1889, the theater had been abandoned for nearly half a century. It quickly became apparent, however, that there were forces in the Bird Cage unconcerned with the passage of time.

While the first visitors to the old theater-turned-museum were treated to artifacts from a time past, many of these early western enthusiasts were far more impressed by the bizarre and frightening phenomena occurring in the building. Early visitors were surprised to hear the sounds of a distant party. Distant voices were singing old folksongs, boisterous peals of men's laughter could be heard faintly and a whiff of cigar smoke could be smelled on the air. Witnesses would head downstairs, convinced that some sort of party was going on in the basement, but all they would find when they got there was the abandoned Poker Room. History's longest poker game was played in this room during the 1880s, running nonstop, so it is said, for eight years, five months and three days. The sounds of distant revelry would stop the moment anyone opened the door to this room, though chilled witnesses would later swear that there was something intangibly eerie about the silent room and its unoccupied chairs—as if, somehow, invisible gamblers were still sitting on them, waiting for everyone to leave before they commenced their game.

Other people claimed to hear the sound of a woman singing faintly in one of the second-floor cribs overlooking the main room. The singing would grow clearer when witnesses ventured up to the second floor, but it would cease before anyone could get too close to any of the cribs. There were other reports as well. People spoke of hearing spur-jangling footsteps walking across the main room on the first floor when there was no one there. Sometimes the disembodied footsteps would come incredibly close to visitors, passing within mere inches of frazzled witnesses, but even then, the phantom presence would remain invisible to human eyes. Or, rather, to *some* people's eyes. For there were also those who claimed to spot the purported phantom as he made his way across the Bird Cage's main room. He appeared as a semi-transparent figure in a black suit, wearing a big black cowboy hat on his head. Witnesses could make out enough to note that he walked with a casual stride, and that his hair was black as pitch, but the apparition has always vanished before anyone could discern much more.

Things at the Bird Cage haven't changed that much since the building was reopened in 1934. Now, as then, many of visitors claim to see and hear inexplicable phenomena. The occurrences themselves have remained remarkably constant over the last 70 years. For the most part, what was reported then is still reported today, giving the Bird Cage Theatre as much of an allure among supernatural enthusiasts as it has with history buffs.

The theater has gotten a good deal of attention from paranormal societies, many of which have worked to clarify the phenomena there. According to some of these societies' investigations, the Bird Cage is every bit as haunted as its past might suggest. While psychics have been able to detect a large confluence of restless souls, more scientifically oriented organizations have amassed a number of photographs and video and audio recordings suggesting that the Bird Cage might indeed house a whole group of ghosts. The Southwest Ghost Hunters' Association has reported that as many as 31 revenants might be haunting the theater.

Angel Brant, a gifted psychic who lives in Mesa, Arizona, doesn't dispute that there are real supernatural entities in the Bird Cage. "There's a lot of ethereal energy in the building. Much of it comes from the objects on display, so many of which transmit the energy of their former owners, and then, of course, a lot of it comes from all the excitement and drama that took place there when it was open, energy like that doesn't just go away." That being said, Angel herself has only ever detected one specific spirit in the Bird Cage.

"The first time I felt his presence was when a good friend and I went to visit. We were walking up to the backstage area on the main floor when we both smelled this really strong cigar odor. It was like there was someone right there smoking a big, stinky cigar, but the only people in the area were my friend and I." The pair went back down to the main floor where they saw the only other person in the theater. "We asked this man if he had been smoking a cigar and he told us that he hadn't. So then we asked him to come up backstage, just to see if he'd smell the same thing." When the trio got back to the area, the cigar smell had completely dissipated, but whoever had been smoking it apparently was still there. "Neither me nor my friend felt anything, but the guy that was there with us suddenly looked really surprised and sort of scared. We followed him back down to the main floor, where he told us that something backstage had been pushing him away by the chest. It was like there was someone there who didn't want him to be backstage."

All three were mystified by the experience until Angel came up with an informative bit of history on the building. "It turns out that there used to be this stage manager who worked backstage," Angel explains, "and during the Bird Cage's busiest time, his job was also to keep the men away from the dancing girls and the women who were in the cribs upstairs." Angel also discovered that this man was scarcely seen without a big, malodorous Mexican cigar jutting from his mouth. Angel is sure that they had encountered the spirit of this stage manager that day. It is fitting that this spirit— who had guarded so many female performers from the male audience when he was alive—would hold back the only male in the trio while allowing the two women to get by. It seems that even in the afterlife, the spirit of this resolute stage manager continues to do his job, keeping the rough rabble of male visitors away from the women. "I sense that this man loved his job," Angel says. "That's why he's there, he loved working at the Bird Cage so much that he hasn't been able to let it go yet."

Ghost of the Bell Union Building

Karen Carter was another person who enjoyed her stay in Tombstone, though she is much more talkative about her time there than the Bird Cage's old stage manager. Currently living in the state of Virginia, Karen moved to Tombstone in 1992 after her family doctor told her the dry Arizona air would relieve her son's asthma. She ended up spending the next three years there, making ends meet waiting on tables at the Bell Union Restaurant in the Bell Union Building on 4th and Fremont. Returning home in 1995, Karen counts her experiences in the Bell Union among her most memorable during her stay in Tombstone.

"I hadn't been working in Bell Union for too long when I got wise to the strange things going on," Karen says today. "It happened one night after closing. Tracy, a friend and coworker, was there with me. We were in the dining room, just about to start up our closing duties when it started."

Karen and Tracy were busy moving chairs when the silverware on each and every table began to shake. At first, the carefully arranged cutlery moved with a barely perceptible vibration, but within a matter of minutes, every fork, knife and spoon in the restaurant were jumping inches off the tables, rattling in a frightful cacophony. "Well, of course, we were terrified," Karen says, "and without really thinking, both of us ran out of the dining room and into the kitchen."

Whatever reprieve the pair were hoping to find there didn't last long. "We weren't in the kitchen for more than a minute or two before the dishwasher door slammed shut and started running all by itself. Me and Tracy were standing right there when it happened. Both of us could see that there was no one in front of the dishwasher." That was when Karen and Tracy decided that they had had enough. The owners lived in an apartment at the back of the building, and the pair ran down the hall to the apartment entrance, banging on the door in frightened desperation. The owners weren't home, but the short time away from the Bell Union restaurant allowed the two women to collect their thoughts.

"Well, after a few minutes out in the hallway, me and Tracy got to laughing at ourselves. We talked about what had just happened, and sort of convinced ourselves that we might've overreacted a little bit." The pair walked carefully back into the restaurant, where they saw that though the dishwasher was still running, the dining room was totally quiet. Relieved that things seemed to have gotten back to normal, Karen and Tracy decided to get back to work. "Well, we ended up not getting much done," Karen says. "We were just getting started when I told Karen that I was going to brew some coffee. The moment I said it, the coffee maker started all by itself. Water just started pouring out of the percolator. There was no pot underneath, and the water was overflowing onto the counter." Too frightened to stop the coffee machine, or even put a pot underneath it, the pair bolted out the front, locked the door behind them and called it a night.

The next morning, Karen expected to be in some trouble when she came into work, seeing as how she and Tracy had left the place in a mess the night before. "Both owners, Jim and Dave, were there when I got to work the next day, cleaning the place up. I was surprised at how good they were taking it, but I was much more surprised at their reaction when I told them what happened the night before."

"So," Jim said to Karen, laughing, "you've met Charlie."

"Charlie," Karen soon found out, was the ghost that had been haunting the Bell Union Building for as long as anyone could remember. Quite a few different businesses had occupied the Bell Union since it was built in the early 1880s. For the first few years it was open, it housed the town's post office. Then it was purchased by a recently arrived Chinese entrepreneur who promptly turned the place into one of Tombstone's seediest establishments. Seedy in 1890s Tombstone would have translated into downright rotten anywhere else, yet such was the reputation of the Bell Union opium den that even some of the town's worst made it a habit to stay away. Thankfully for the law, however, the drug house wasn't open for long.

The opium den's proprietor met his end soon after he opened the place. According to legend, it happened while he and a friend were all juiced up on opium. Someone got the idea that a knife-throwing contest would be a lot of fun, an idea that found the two opium-addled men in complete agreement. One thing led to another and in all the time it took for a knife to fly across the room, the Bell Union's owner found himself on the floor with a bowie knife jutting from his chest. He would be dead before the opium in his blood stream wore off.

While the opium owner faded in Tombstone's memory as quickly as weeds grew over his grave, everyone who worked at the Bell Union was reminded of him on a near-weekly basis. For they were convinced that this man's spirit was haunting their restaurant. His activities were sporadic and unpredictable. Sometimes, his ghost would be content enough to unravel the toilet paper, open and close doors or fool around with the lights. But on other occasions, his behavior would be far more dramatic.

Karen recalls her most frightening run-in with Charlie: "Well, it was the end of another shift, and me and Tracy were in late, cleaning the place up. The place was totally closed up; I mean, there was no one in there besides Tracy and me, and all the doors were locked. So we were cleaning up in the dining room, again, when this man suddenly appears out of nowhere. He was a Chinese man, but he wasn't wearing the clothes that so many of the Chinese seemed to wear back then: he looked just like a cowboy, dressed up in a dirty old outfit, with a long coat and a banged-up cowboy hat."

Karen and Tracy had become accustomed to Charlie's pranks, but this sighting was more than either of them had bargained for. This man looked as real as anyone walking down Allen Street on any given day. "He walked around the bar, looked at us once and then went on through the swinging doors that led to the back hallway." Karen and Tracy may have gotten used to the strange things that were going on in the restaurant; this incident, however, was too hard to overlook. Trying to convince herself that this man was an intruder, Karen called the police. Yet the ensuing investigation only confirmed that inexplicable things were afoot at the Bell Union.

"When the police got there, they found no evidence of a forced entry," Karen says. "All the doors were still locked and intact, and the Chinese cowboy that we saw was nowhere to be found. He wasn't in the back hallway, in either of the bathrooms or in the kitchen. And the door to Jim's apartment was still locked, so they decided he wasn't in there either." But the police were wrong in thinking that this intruder would be impeded by any lock or door. "When Jim got home later on that night, his place was completely trashed," Karen says. "His clothes were strewn all over the place; his furniture was upended; his papers were everywhere. The place was a complete mess."

Yet Jim knew better than to call the authorities. Years of experience with Charlie had forced him to accept the occasional fit of domestic carnage. Karen, as well, learned to put up with the Chinese ghost. Though Charlie would never again appear in front of her the way he did that night, he always made sure that not too much time elapsed without another prank. Most were minor incidents. In the three years that Karen worked in the Bell Union, a week never went by without the radio changing stations by itself, candles lighting on their own or water running by itself. Karen eventually got used to Charlie and often addressed him like she would anyone else in the Bell Union. And unlike the reaction of many people to encounters with the supernatural, Karen laughs when she looks back at her experiences in Tombstone. "Charlie just wasn't ready to say 'bye' to the Bell Union. I guess that's why his spirit is still there today."

Murder on Skyline Drive

The haunting on Skyline Drive is one of the lesser-known ghost stories in Tombstone's heavily chronicled past. While thousands of tourists and curiosity seekers flock to famous haunted sites such as Big Nose Kate's Saloon and the Bird Cage every year, the haunted house on Skyline Drive gets very little attention. That is just as well as far as the current owners of the home are concerned, for they are none too eager to sacrifice their privacy for the sake of putting another haunted location on Tombstone's supernatural register.

Thus Angel Brant is a little bit guarded when she talks about the stately old house up on the hill on Skyline Drive. "Most of us can only imagine what it would take to live in a place so actively haunted by the spirits of the dead," Angel says, "never mind putting up with the widespread attention that this sort of thing brings on." So even though Angel is more than willing to talk about her ongoing investigation of this home, all she will reveal about its location is the street that it lies on.

"Back in the 1880s, one of Tombstone's wealthiest assayers used to live in this house," Angel says. "This was the man that the miners would come to with the ore they dug up in exchange for pay." Very little information survives on this assayer. It is known that he lived in the house with his wife and his daughter and that he supervised a few of the mining operations around town, but Angel has found no written record of his name or background. All she knows about him is what she's been able to gather during her psychic investigations. "I keep getting an impression of the name Cliverson," Angel says. "I'm pretty sure this was the assayer's family name."

"Sometime in the 1880s, Mr. Cliverson fired a man named John Hicks, who worked in one of his mines." Angel can't say for certain why Hicks was fired, but given what followed, it's apparent that the miner wasn't at all happy about it. A few days later, an angry and inebriated John Hicks came knocking on Cliverson's door, looking for money he felt he was owed.

"Well, Cliverson wasn't home," Angel says, "but his wife and his eight-year-old daughter were." Mrs. Cliverson opened the door and found herself looking into the eyes of a man lost to fury. Hicks kicked the door open and sauntered inside, roaring about just desserts and money that was owed him. Terrified, Mrs. Cliverson tried telling the drunk miner that her husband wasn't there, that he was out working at one of the mines, but her words were meaningless to him; the man was beyond reason. In a fit of homicidal madness, Hicks exacted his inhuman vengeance, assaulting Mrs. Cliverson and then stabbing her to death. Just as he was leaving, he turned to see the Cliversons' daughter staring at her mother in mortal fear. Hicks turned his knife on the eight-year-old. And then he was gone.

The strange goings-on in the house today find their roots in this horrific sequence of events that took place over 100 years ago. "I've felt the vibrations of the little girl," Angel says. "I've felt her presence while sitting on the front porch. I could feel her fear and the pain of being stabbed." But that's only what Angel had divined during her psychic investigations. Another, far more dramatic, phenomenon occurs on the front deck. Angel describes her experience sitting on the porch with a trace of awe in her voice. "The porch, it rains slag: little fragments of rock—they come out of the overhang and shower all over the patio floor, they form on the walls and on the steps."

Angel believes the little girl is responsible for this bizarre occurrence. "I think that this is the girl's way of keeping men away. Because the time that I saw it happen, the slag rained all around me, but I didn't feel any of it—what I did feel was her being stabbed violently. I got a real impression of this poor girl's fear." According to Angel, this falling slag is the girl's defense mechanism against males she doesn't know. More than one male visitor to the house has been welcomed with a fine mist of falling slag.

Why the front porch? In all probability, the raining rock phenomenon used to occur inside the house, before previous owners' renovations turned the living room into the porch. While no one will ever know what motivated these renovations, we might imagine how difficult it must have been to be constantly cleaning slag off the living room floor. Could it be that residents of the house made the living room into a porch to keep the mysterious rock from collecting inside? Or perhaps they hoped whatever force was haunting the room would depart when the room was turned into an outdoor area. They very well might have known that the girl and her mother were killed in the living room and could have come to the conclusion that the ghost of one of the two was responsible for the phenomenon.

If so, they would quickly learn that all they solved with the renovations was their cleaning problem. For the spirit of the girl continues to rain down slag on the same part of the house where she met her end, continuing on, perhaps, for as long as her ghost continues to relive the last brutal moments of her short life.

2
Cowboys and Indians

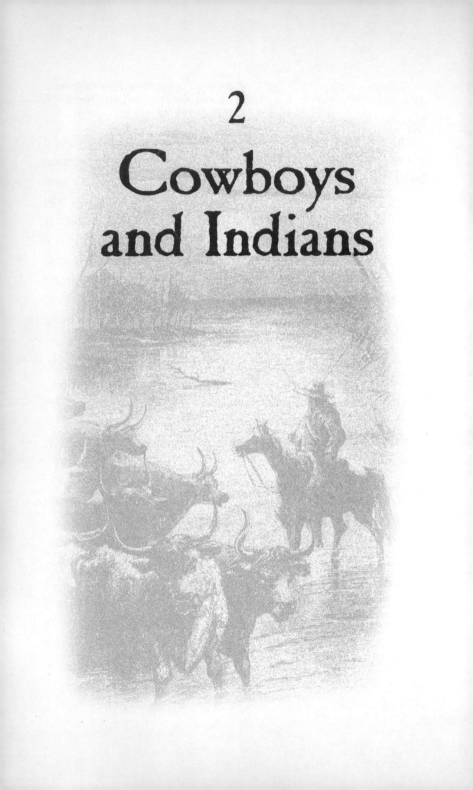

Mystery of the Frog Lake Vision

With his tired old eyes Big Bear looked at the forms of the Cree braves gathered around the roaring fire. The assembled warriors writhed and stomped as they bellowed their threats into the starry night; they bragged about counting coups and how many scalps they were going to take; they sang songs of their proud past. Strengthened by years of hunger, injustice and want, the young men of the Cree reserve were ready for the worst, just as they were fully prepared to deliver it to the people they called their enemies. It was the evening of April 1, 1885, on the banks of the North Saskatchewan River, and tomorrow, blood would flow.

Only Big Bear, one of their most revered leaders, was uncertain. Not that he was afraid. Throughout his younger years, the Plains Cree had been at war with the Blackfoot Confederacy, and Big Bear had proven himself with rifle and hatchet more than once. But those were different days, when the buffalo still roamed the plains in massive herds and the Cree warriors were proud and strong. The men he saw before him now were gaunt and desperate. They were warriors fighting for a rapidly fading way of life, and no matter how many battles they won against white men, Big Bear knew that their stomachs would still be empty. Louis Riel's Métis had just risen up in the east, and the Indians of Frog Lake Reserve, having just gotten wind of the Métis victory, were inspired to do the same, but Big Bear found it hard to be joyful. He knew. Bloodshed wouldn't bring back the buffalo. Bloodshed wouldn't stop the white man from coming west.

The Plains Cree war chief, Wandering Spirit, wasn't inclined to agree. "In the morning, I am going to eat two-legged meat!" the warrior roared at the assembled men as he stood before the bonfire. "If you don't want to join me, then go home and put on your wives' dresses!" It was then that the Indians' shouts of approval were interrupted by another voice, the voice of a woman, which suddenly came from the darkness.

"Then it is best that all of you learn to wear dresses, for no good will come of murdering the white man tomorrow." Everyone got quiet as an old Cree woman stepped in front of Wandering Spirit. She stood no higher than the war chief's chest but looked firmly into his eyes and spoke sternly, as if she was addressing a child. "I woke two nights ago from a dream, a terrible vision, where a church burned and eight men lay on bloody ground. A white man rode in on a white horse, and when he raised his hand, defeat fell on our people. I tell you now that when we see this man, we will all be doomed."

Everyone around the fire fell silent. The woman stood straight, unaffected by the weight of the eyes that fell upon her. Wandering Spirit broke the silence with a booming laugh. "Big Bear!" he hollered into the crowd. "Does this woman belong to you? Her words sound like they come from your mouth, our far-too-careful leader."

Big Bear's response came quietly from the darkness. "I have never once seen this woman before." In fact, no one knew who the mysterious harbinger was. She'd appeared out of nowhere on the Frog Lake Reserve early that morning, shortly before the War Dance was called together. All day, she had been spreading the message of her vision throughout the reservation. If many of the Cree took her message to heart

Wandering Spirit was one of the braves who witnessed a terrifying apparition in the sky.

during the daylight hours, the braves gathered around Wandering Spirit that night proved far less tolerant.

Wandering Spirit disregarded the bearer of the ominous message with a simple laugh, and the Cree woman was roughly removed from the circle of ready warriors. Early the next morning, on April 2, 1885, the Cree warriors descended on the small settlement of Frog Lake, executing eight residents of the frontier community right in front of Frog Lake's humble little church, just as the Indian woman had foretold. But Wandering Spirit's party was resolved to action, and not one of them bothered to talk about the woman's vision. Taking two women captive, the braves headed east down the North Saskatchewan, toward Fort Pitt, which they intended to destroy. The Cree seer, adamant to stop the attack on the Hudson's Bay Company trading post, set off with them. She warned them every hour of every day, approaching Wandering Spirit himself and warning him against any further action. "I know the great Wandering Spirit has a proud heart which seeks vengeance," she said, "but this will amount to nothing. We shall be defeated when we see the man on the white horse, as will Louis Riel to the east."

Somewhere along the way, Wandering Spirit got fed up with this Cree Cassandra's warnings, and when he did, he acted with the hardest part of his heart. Ordering five warriors to get rid of her, Wandering Spirit was as impassive as stone when the poor woman was dragged away from the party and axed to death. We may never know how deeply, if at all, this woman's prophecy affected the war party, for they ended up attacking Fort Pitt two weeks later, easily managing to drive the small garrison out. But her words must have surely come back to them a month and a half later. During the twilight of May 13, just before the Cree found themselves in a pitched gunfight with General Strange and his troop of North-West Mounted Police (NWMP), the man on the white horse appeared.

According to legend, he appeared in the sky just as the sun was beginning to set. One moment, there was only the sunset and the crimson clouds; the next, the clouds parted like curtains, and the Frog Lake Church was perched in the sky above them all like some sort of celestial theater. Everyone in Wandering Spirit's band stared in awe, looking up at the sky as the murders they had visited on the settlers at Frog Lake were replayed, one by one, before their very eyes. The moment the last settler was struck down, a strange rider appeared on the scene. He was an old man dressed all in white atop a white horse. The scene in the sky began to dissolve even as the man galloped across it, and when there was nothing there but sky once more, the old man remained. He came galloping down on the bewildered braves, pointing an accusing finger earthward as he came. Each of the assembled braves shook in terror at the sight of this apparition, certain that they had angered some force that was beyond them. Yet just as he reached the earth, the old man vanished, leaving the ruffled group of warriors standing dumbstruck.

Quarrels broke out between the braves almost immediately after the man disappeared. Some men recalled the vision of the woman they had killed and insisted that they bury their hatchets, while the more steadfast among them argued that their struggle wasn't over, that they feared hunger much more than a vision in the sky. But the damage was done, and when the NWMP engaged Wandering Spirit's warriors at Frenchman's Butte the next day, the warriors' hearts were not in the battle. It would be the last battle of the North-West Rebellion of 1885. Almost every leader who played a part in the insurrection was apprehended, from Big Bear and Poundmaker to Louis Riel himself.

As for the identity of the Cree woman who foresaw the vision and the man in white who came down from the skies, these must forever remain a mystery in the folklore of the Canadian West. No figure in Indian mysticism matched the description of the man in white, and nothing was ever discovered about the woman who appeared at the Frog Lake War Dance. Nevertheless, to this very day it has been said that the old man has been spotted along the North Saskatchewan River near Frenchman's Butte, descending from the sky and vanishing just before he touches the earth, though there are no more rebellious Cree braves to look at him and tremble.

Legend of the Qu'Appelle River Valley

The Qu'Appelle River runs through southern Saskatchewan, a long ribbon of water flowing eastward through the wide prairie on its timeless and much-storied course. Flanked on either side by lush river valley, the Qu'Appelle River has been a focus of prairie life for as long as there has been life on the prairie. The broad and verdant valley was a haven for man and animal alike, allowing life to flourish in the desiccated short-grass prairie of southern Saskatchewan. A breeding ground for bison, deer and antelope, the river was also valuable territory to the Plains Indians of the region, who came to depend upon the abundant game and shelter of the Qu'Appelle River valley for survival.

The first fur traders to arrive in the region were the French *voyageurs*, bold 18th-century pathfinders who took European commerce into the Canadian hinterland. For these intrepid traders, the Qu'Appelle was a passage to western lands and their untapped fur markets. When these Frenchmen first

In the early 1700s, a young Cree man traveling by canoe heard a ghostly voice, which ultimately spelled tragedy for him.

paddled their canoes up the Qu'Appelle in the late 1700s, they were greeted by friendly Plains Cree, all too eager to trade beaver pelts for European rifles, metal pots, beads and blankets. The North West Company built a trading post called Fort Espérance on the southern bank of the Qu'Appelle in 1787 and soon established lasting relationships with the local Cree.

The legend of the Qu'Appelle was born not long after the Nor'Westers set up shop. It was a simple enough tale, but one that left such a lasting impression on the traders of Espérance that it put the Qu'Appelle River on the map…literally. The name of the river itself, *Qu'Appelle*, French for "who calls?", is the translation of the Cree name for the same prairie stream: "Katepwa-Cipi."

"Katepwa-Cipi?" These were the words a young Cree brave called into the darkened sky on a moonless night sometime in the early 18th century, many years before Fort Espérance was built. This warrior was alone, sitting in his canoe, motionless, listening anxiously for a response to the terse question he had just asked of the night. None came.

There was only the sound of his ragged breathing, his pounding heart and the gentle waters of the river as they lapped against his canoe. The brave was tired. He had been rowing upstream for five days, paddling straight through the night for the last two. His arms, motionless now for the first time in 48 hours, began to grow numb and heavy. He sat still for a few moments longer, straining to hear the voice he thought he just heard. It was *her* voice; he could have sworn it—low and tender on the river, calling out his name.

He did not wait too much longer. "I could sit on this river for a day and night trying to hear her voice," the brave said to himself, "but it still would not bring me any nearer to the woman who is calling." Resolved to rowing once again, the young man willed his deadened arms into motion. But just before he was about to plunge his paddle back into the water, he heard her again—*her* voice, the voice of his long-missed lover, calling out his name on the river, as if she were on a canoe just beyond the darkness. "Katepwa-Cipi?" he called out again, this time his voice quavering with an unmistakable twinge of fear.

He had left in late spring that year, leaving his people to travel east for reasons now lost to us. By all accounts, it was to be a long journey, keeping him away from home for the entire summer. But before he left, he promised his lover that they would marry when he returned. He made this promise with a firm and ardent heart; no one in the tribe doubted the young man's passion, and all expected to see him again before the days shortened and the leaves abandoned their boughs.

The young man was determined to hold to his vow. When the first fitful gusts of a north wind swept over the prairie, he concluded his business and turned his canoe to the west, intent on getting back home before frost settled over the morning grass. So it was that he began his arduous journey home. Possessed by a Herculean determination, he traveled throughout the day and deep into the night, allowing himself only the briefest rest from the near-constant paddling. Whenever weariness threatened to get the better of him, he would just bring the smiling face of his betrothed to mind, and his limbs would become charged with new energy.

Yet while the brave's journey home was rushed and strenuous, it was also strangely joyless. Every paddle stroke towards home brought greater anxiety; he began to feel unsure of what might be waiting for him when he got there. For reasons he couldn't understand, the thought of his marriage began to seem like an impossibility, a wishful dream from long ago. Though his arms were still strong and his eyesight keen, his heart started to feel old; inside, he had aged. His love for his woman had not diminished, but as he got closer to home, the brave began to experience increasing difficulty recalling the details of his fiancée's face. Trying his best to ignore the creeping fear that something horrible had happened, the brave paddled even harder, though his inexplicably old and wounded heart was whispering horrible things to his disbelieving mind.

The brave was just half a day's travel from home when he heard his fiancée's voice on the river. He hadn't stopped for two days and a night and was planning to row straight through the night again, hoping to be home by the coming sunrise. That was the plan, but then he heard her voice and his resolution froze, turning his hope to fear and his limbs to stone. It was her voice. She had called his name.

He sat in the canoe, sitting still, trying to calm his labored breath, listening for any words that might follow, all the while unsure if he could believe his own ears. Squinting into the darkness ahead, he looked for the woman who had called his name, but there was nothing there besides the river, the valley and a swollen orange moon rising over the hills behind him.

"Katepwa-Cipi?" he finally called out in his Cree tongue. *Who is calling?* No one answered. A few more moments passed in silence before the brave decided that, voice in the darkness or no, remaining still would not get him home any faster. Reaching forward, he was just about to dip his paddle into the water when her voice sounded out of the darkness again—this time almost pleading, calling his name.

A bone-chilling fear filled the young brave. "Katepwa-Cipi?" he called again, his trembling voice nearly failing him. No answer came. "Qu'Appelle?" he asked again, this time in French, thinking, perhaps, that a canoe full of *voyageurs* might be in the darkness just ahead. How these French fur traders would know his name, or why they would be calling his name, were questions he wasn't interested in asking. "Qu'Appelle?" he called out again, this time louder. No response.

"Qu'Appelle!?" he cried out again, this time yelling at the top of his voice. The third time he asked, the young brave finally got his answer. It came from the cliffs that loomed on either side of the valley: his echo, sounding small and desperate in the huge prairie night. "Qu'Appelle!?" it asked back of the young man on the river. Only then, when he heard his own diminished voice over the river, did he realize that he was actually alone. For reasons he would never understand, this realization filled him with dread.

Redoubling his efforts, the brave dipped his oar back into the water and his canoe lunged up the river. He finished the last leg of his journey the fastest, but the sight that greeted him when he arrived confirmed his worst fears. Sacred fires were burning all along the riverbank, fires that were lit to ease a departed soul's journey to the Creator. The young man did not need to ask for whom these fires were lit; somehow he knew, beyond any doubt, that they were lit for the woman he loved.

Without a word, he walked to her teepee, where her body still lay. The sight of her motionless form filled his heart with grief, and he looked to her friends and family, who were gathered around her in silence. "When did she die?" the heartbroken brave asked.

"She fell ill less than one moon ago," the woman's mother answered. "We tried every medicine we knew, but nothing took away the sickness. She gave up her spirit this last night, just as the moon was rising in the east." The despondent woman looked away from the warrior as she spoke her last words to him. "She called out your name then. She asked for you twice before she died. It was the last word she spoke."

"I know," the man responded, "I heard her." The brave, overcome with despair, told the old woman the story of the night before. Then, without another word, he turned and ran out of the teepee through the Cree village and into his canoe, driving his vessel back into the river. No one would ever see the young Cree brave again.

But that would not be the end of this tragic tale. Soon after he disappeared, many Indians and Métis who happened to be on the river late at night claimed to hear a voice, far-flung and small, as if coming from a great distance. It only ever said one thing, asking the same sad question of the indifferent river. "Qu'Appelle?" the voice asked, once, twice, three times, before falling silent. The mysterious voice was consistently heard throughout the years, until the local Indians took to calling the river itself the Qu'Appelle. Traders of the North West Company were told of the legend of the Qu'Appelle early in the 19th century, and the river became known by the same haunting question among eastern populations as well. The famed Canadian poet E. Pauline Johnson would commemorate the story with her romantic ode, "The Legend of the Qu'Appelle Valley."

And it is said to this very day that if one is canoeing through the right stretch of the Qu'Appelle River when a full moon is shining, the ancient question might still be heard, faintly drifting down the river on a gentle breeze. "Qu'Appelle?" the young brave asks, still searching for his long-lost love.

The Lost Tribe
of the Rocky Mountains

They do not appear on anthropologists' lists of Indian bands, archeological records or the history books. Nothing in the records of formal academic study suggests they exist. No archeological remains or cultural relics indicating the passage of the legendary tribe have ever been dug out of American soil. Nevertheless, the People of the Snake have long occupied a place in the mythos of the American Indian. According to legend, this elusive band thrived in the upper reaches of the American Rockies, living in alpine meadows and deep tunnels within the craggy mountain peaks. Not to be mistaken for the Shoshone, or Snake, Nation, which occupied much of the land around the Rockies, this group of mountain dwellers never waged war against a neighboring tribe or traded a single item with any white entrepreneur.

In fact, the Snake People were seen only at night, and even then, terrified eyewitnesses saw them only as moving shadows and gleaming eyes darting through the darkness, there one moment, gone the next. No one believed these sightings to be auspicious. For in addition to being mysterious, the People of the Snake were thought to be evil. Believed to live in small groups dotted across the mountains, each clan took care of one enormous viper that it worshipped like a god. Living for the sole purpose of finding suitable sacrifices for the gigantic snakes they tended to, this group of Indians visited others only when they needed a living person for their gruesome rites.

Tribes situated around the Rockies had the most trouble with the Snake People because they regularly sneaked into their settlements and made off with a few of their young and their old. Fighting would usually break out if these malicious interlopers were spotted, but while there would be no shortage of dead Indians after these nocturnal confrontations, no one was ever known to have struck down one of the Snake People. Those who fought them and lived would talk about how they were nearly invisible and moved as fast as a darting snake. Yet these encounters were nothing compared to those nights when members of this serpentine tribe would come down from the mountains with their enormous vipers slithering behind them.

On such nights, the vipers themselves attacked Indian settlements, creeping up silently on a band's horse pens and attacking silently, in a dart and a flash, killing all the prized animals with volumes of deadly venom. Often, these attacks would come in complete silence, only to be discovered the next morning. And those who did look upon these massive vipers doing their grisly work were none too eager to fight them. More often than not, Indians would see only two enormous serpent eyes staring from the darkness for an instant before the snake would dart off into the darkness. Efficient as they were at taking down horses, these legendary snakes would rarely attack humans.

The problems with the Snake People took a back seat when white men began flooding into the American West. If raiding Snake People and their giant vipers were scary enough, the arriving wave of white men bent on the destruction of Indian populations posed a far greater problem, and the Snake People were largely forgotten as Indians indigenous to the Rocky Mountains were either killed or concentrated in reservations.

It was apparent that the Snake People did not suffer the same fate as their age-old victims. For a while nothing was heard of them, but it wasn't long before horrifying stories about enormous serpents and shadows in the night began emerging from small pockets of settlers in and around the Rockies. No one knows where the Snake People went while the white men took over the countryside, and how it was that they managed to avoid detection; nevertheless, over time it became evident that the settlers would have no more success with the nocturnal predators than the Indians.

Early miners, ranchers and farmers living near the mountains would mysteriously lose their babies and their elderly in the night. Ranchers often woke to find too many of their cattle dead in the morning—their animals gouged by two enormous holes and filled with enough venom to kill an elephant. Settlers lost livestock. Those unfortunate few that laid eyes on the perpetrators of these crimes would never forget it, and stories of darting shadows and enormous serpents began circulating through the West again.

If the Indians knew about the return of the Snake People, they said very little about it, perhaps hoping that the evil in the mountains would drive the white settlers away. It did not. Instead, it seemed as if the Snake People were retreating into their mountains as the years passed, coming out less and less frequently to terrorize the people around them. By the end of the 1800s, run-ins with the mysterious mountain dwellers were rarer than tornadoes in San Francisco.

But this isn't to say that they ceased all together. In his book *Ghosts of the Old West*, Earl Murray narrates his account of a young man who spotted a gigantic snake one night in the summer of 1982. According to Murray, this man, an Apache Indian going by the pseudonym "Mahlan," was driving to his sister's home somewhere in the central Rockies when he saw the beast. A few miles from his sister's home, Mahlan got out of his car to open a gate barring the road when a stifling odor filled the air; Mahlan recognized the smell of a pit viper. Just after he got back in his car, the snake appeared—two narrow yellow eyes sitting about 3 feet apart in a head he couldn't make out clearly in the darkness. Suddenly filled with terror, Mahlan was able only to stare at the creature in fear, convinced that these would be his final moments. And then the snake turned and slithered away, vanishing in the night. Mahlan drove to his sister's ranch as fast as his car would take him.

Telling her about his experience on the road later that night, Mahlan was surprised to learn that his sister and brother-in-law's cattle had been dying for quite some time, their poisoned carcasses turning up along the river's edge. It was then that Mahlan's sister told him about the Snake People, how she had seen them on their ranch at nights, dark silhouettes darting about their compound.

It seems, then, that the old Indian legend persists, if not with the same vehemence that it once did. Who are the Snake People? Where did they go? Where do they reside today? Plain curiosity might impel us to find answers, while simple wisdom might advise us to just accept. Given the fear and death that always seemed to have followed them wherever they go, perhaps it is enough to be thankful that they are not as active as they once were, and to be hopeful that things will remain this way.

The 101 Ranch

They say you can hear them, at night, off Highway 177, on a wide-open stretch of prairie just south of Ponca City. Cowboys—crooning over the nocturnal din of the plains, over the crickets, bullfrogs and coyotes, drifting in on a wind from nowhere. Sometimes the song is a cowboy waltz, with harmonicas, a piano and guitars lilting through a pleasant melody. On other occasions, traces of an old western ballad, where one man sings a haunting melody, are accompanied only by the strains of minor chords on an acoustic guitar. There are other voices as well, and the sounds of distant laughter and clapping; some have heard dozens of voices raised in unison singing one of the classic range songs of all time: "Whoopee ti yi yo, git along, little dogies, It's your misfortune and none of my own."

The distant sounds of this mysterious hoedown have been heard for about half a century now. Motorists taking a rest stop, tarrying picnickers and hitchhikers stranded along 177 late at night have all reported hearing the sounds of an antiquated party countless times over the years, making the cowpunchers' celebration near Ponca City one of Oklahoma's most enduring mysteries.

A mystery, yes, but the Oklahomans in Kay County have not much doubt as to the origin of this strange soiree, though many people might prefer to leave the matter unanswered after hearing the popular explanation from local Sooners. It is a story that defies the conventional wisdom of our age. Who are these revelers? They are ghosts.

And not just any ghosts. For the sounds of the hoedown are always heard in the same area, off Highway 177, just south of Ponca City, the exact past location of the legendary 101 Ranch.

Today, there is only a picnic area and a National Historic Landmark where the headquarters for the world-famous 101 Ranch Wild West Show used to be. Established in 1879 by Colonel George W. Miller, the 101 Ranch—its name came from the sprawling 101,000 acres it was spread over—was an immense operation. At its peak, it contained a fully staffed school, general store, hotel, café, magazine, newspaper, smithy, dairy, meat-packing plant and oil refinery. Home to about 3000 American citizens, the 101 Ranch was one of the biggest ranching outfits in the West. George Miller's three sons took over the ranch when the colonel passed away in 1903. Under their management, the 101 Ranch became famous across the country.

In 1900, Wild West shows were big business. Pioneered by Buffalo Bill Cody during the late 1800s, they were immensely popular productions by the turn of the century and sold out pavilions around the world. The Millers drew from the talented hands they had working for them, and by 1905, put together what was considered to be the greatest Wild West Show in the country. Its very first show was a roaring success, and the 101 Ranch Wild West Show maintained its popularity for over two decades, traveling across the United States and even across the Atlantic to Europe. They were good times for the Millers: money was coming in, everyone wanted to be in their production and the Whitehouse, their three-story white stucco ranch home, became a meeting place for every colorful character that whirled a lasso in the state of Oklahoma.

The brothers' splendid ranch headquarters was almost always packed with the best showmen from all the Wild West

The 101 Ranch Wild West Show was popular for over two decades.

shows proliferating across the state. Celebrities such as Pawnee Bill, Buck Jones and the renowned cowboy-philosopher Will Rogers were regulars at the Whitehouse. It was said that every weekend, the sounds of merriment coming from the Miller ranch could be heard for miles around. Gathering beside an enormous campfire, the revelers sang, danced and shared stories about their innumerable escapades on the ranches and stages across the country.

The good times lasted well into the 1920s. After the Millers added silent movies to their arena of operations, the business got more successful year after year, and by 1925, it seemed that things couldn't possibly get better for the 101 Ranch. But they could definitely get worse. In 1927, Joe, the eldest Miller brother, died of carbon monoxide poisoning; two years later, the middle son, Zack, was killed in a car accident. That left the youngest, George, to manage the entire ranch by himself, a task he may well have been up to if the onset of the Great Depression didn't ravage the family business. By 1931, the 101 Ranch was financially ruined. In 1932, the Whitehouse was torn down, the property was divided up and the parcels of land were auctioned off to prospective farmers.

The coming years brought a great many new developments throughout Oklahoma and the world, but those pioneer entertainers who entertained on horseback with gun and lasso were past their heyday. Wild West shows became a thing of the past, and the men and woman who starred in the expositions were growing old. One by one, they passed on. Will Rogers died in an airplane accident in 1935 in Point Barrow, Alaska. But it wasn't until 1952, when George Miller passed on in his Texas home, that the bizarre reports of an invisible party began circulating around Ponca City.

Lone motorists running errands out of town were the first to hear the sounds of revelry carrying on the prairie wind. When word got out that something strange was afoot south of town, groups of teenagers began taking trips out on weekend evenings, hoping to hear the strains of folk music drift in from the darkness; many of them were not disappointed. Farmers, townsfolk, hitchhikers, curiosity seekers, paranormal enthusiasts...with each visitor the tale of the haunted ranch grew until the entire state came to know of the phantom hoedown in Kay County. And the sounds are said to still continue today, jovial laughter and music coming from somewhere around where the Whitehouse once stood.

Indeed, the first and last great actors of the drama of the Wild West seem intent on continuing what now appears to be an ageless celebration. Who knows? Maybe in the spirit world they inhabit, the buffalo still roam over the Great Plains, the American Indians are fierce and free and the range is still open all the way from southern Texas to the cattle towns of Kansas. Or maybe they're living in an eternal present where there are still throngs of people willing to pay good money and sit in a pavilion to watch them reenact the romance of a time when the West was truly wild. Whatever the case, the party that began almost 80 years ago continues yet, testament that not all ghosts are tortured moaning souls obsessed with the injustices of their earthly years.

Ghost Riders
of the Neches River

Eight cowboys sat on impatient horses, squinting through
the blazing mid-afternoon light at the lone farmhouse on
the plain. They were sore, tired and in bad humor, each of
them festering over the ugly truth of the upcoming months—
a long stretch of hard, dusty days, which would end only
after they had driven their herd of 3000 Texas longhorn to
the stockyards in Abilene, Kansas. But if the thought of the
trail ahead did little to cheer their prickly dispositions, the
sight of the small wooden house before them roused an even
uglier ire.

Farmers and cowboys were natural enemies during the
early days of the range. Cattlemen depended on the unob-
structed expanse of the plains to drive their herds from their
grazing grounds in Texas to Kansan cattle towns, but ambitious homesteaders saw the same tract as potential farmland.
Frontier farmers who fenced off their plots not only deprived
cowboys of grazing land for their cattle, but they also
obstructed the movement of the Texan herds north. So as far
as these eight cowboys were concerned, the innocent-looking
farmhouse on the bank of Texas' Neches River was a personal
attack on their livelihood.

The eight men looked at the solitary farmhouse for long
moments as the enormous herd of cattle gathered behind
them. Four more cowboys rode up from the rear of the herd,
their bandanas tied up around their faces and their clothes
caked with dust and sweat. "What's the holdup?" one of the
four riders asked.

An engraving of Texas longhorns crossing a stream in 1867. Ranching and farming often came into conflict during the time of the cattle drive.

The trail boss spit his tobacco into the Neches River and nodded at the homestead ahead. "Looks like some sodbuster decided to set up."

Two or three of the cowpunchers uttered curses under their breaths. Another man fiddled with the handle of his shooting iron. "Well, what the hell we gonna do about this?" one of the masked riders asked the trail boss. "This man's fence goes as far as I can see."

"Damn these dirt diggers," the wrangler next to the trail boss growled as he looked down the length of the fence. "I reckon we oughta teach this man a lesson."

The cowboys were silent, dwelling over fantasies of punishment, when the farmer came striding out of his home. Obviously scared and angry, the man was brandishing a double barrel Remington and spouting all sorts of unflattering epithets at the cattlemen, promising the worst to each and every one if they didn't turn their herd around.

None of the riders was in the least bit impressed by this show of bravado. The desperation boiling beneath was all too apparent. They stared through the fence at the livid farmer for a few moments longer before the trail boss gave his order. "Let's run this fool over."

Flicking the reins of his horse, the trail boss cast one look at the men in his outfit before galloping to the back of the herd. Not one of them hesitated. Taking their positions around their cattle, the cowboys quickly whipped the herd into an agitated frenzy. The farmer, realizing what was about to happen, ran back into his home, desperately urging his family to get out. But by then, it was too late.

In the next moment, the entire herd burst through the farmer's fence. The homesteader emerged from his house again and managed to empty both barrels of his shotgun into the oncoming stampede just before he was trampled. The herd went over him and stormed toward his one-room farmhouse, where his wife and two children were huddled together in terror, their whispered supplications to a merciful God drowned out by the roar of the stampeding beasts. When the herd hit the house, beams, planks and glass came apart like so many cards and matchsticks. In a few short minutes the entire homestead was reduced to a flattened pile of debris. None survived.

According to legend, not one of the cowboys expressed an iota of remorse at this inhuman deed. They arrived in Abilene early that fall, whooping it up with the rest of the Texas cowpunchers at trail's end. Some of them even bragged about the incident to their confederates, throwing back whiskey and laughing about the look on the plowman's face when their steers crashed through his fence. It became the story of the season around the saloons that year, providing the men of that outfit with a morbid cachet among many of their hardhearted companions.

Staying on in Abilene for just over a month, the cowboys remained until the awe and envy lavished on them by their fellow Texans began to thin out. By October, most cowpunchers had gone back to their southern ranches, and Abilene suddenly resembled a slightly overpopulated ghost town. It was then, when the cowboys packed up and headed home themselves, that they became aware of the price of their atrocious glory.

Hailed as heroes in Abilene for one month in 1870, the cowboys of that cursed outfit would never enjoy another peaceful moment after they crossed back into their home state. For the rest of their days they were haunted by horrible visions and nightmares. Terrifying herds of angry bulls with burning eyes, smoking nostrils and sharpened horns stampeded through their dreams, leaving a cloud of burning dust along a blood red Neches River. The dead family, decomposed and mutilated, often appeared right in front of them during waking hours, standing silently for a few moments before vanishing into thin air as quickly as they came. The repeated appearance of these phantasms made the once-stalwart cowpunchers into a group of quivering wretches. Unable to work another cattle drive, none of them lived long after they returned to Texas in 1870.

Within five years, all of them were dead. Causes of death varied from gunfights to suicide. One man drank himself to death, throwing back the harshest rotgut he could find until his body just gave up. Another, suddenly and inexplicably unable to stomach any morsel of food, simply stopped eating. The trail boss, his pale face frozen into a look of absolute horror, was found face down on the left bank of the Neches River, near the former homestead of the farmer they had killed. What had brought the trail boss to the scene of the crime? What terrifying entity had killed him without leaving so much as a mark?

The last cowboy in the outfit died in 1875; not long after that, the Ghost Riders began to appear on the Neches River. Specifics of their first appearance have been lost over the years. No one can say what the date was or who had seen them first, but the sighting itself has been preserved countless times in the local folklore.

They came just as the sun was sinking low on the horizon, when the immense Texan sky was a scarlet-streaked dome and the Neches ran red like a river of blood to the southeast. It may have been a lone local testing the waters with a fishing rod; perhaps it was a group of ranch hands taking a walk with a bottle of hooch after a hard day of roping and branding. Whoever it was, we can only imagine the reaction when the ground beneath began to rumble, and the whole landscape started to shake. Up above, on the southern horizon, a group of what looked to be thick red clouds suddenly appeared, moving north at great speed. In the span of a few seconds, the clouds were overhead and were no longer clouds but a herd of angry cattle, driven forward by 12 masked cowboys. They roared over the Neches River in a terrible rush, the whole landscape shaking in their wake. And then, in the next instant, they were gone. They vanished suddenly in the dim evening sky, leaving not a trace of their passing.

Since that first appearance in 1875, the Ghost Riders of the Neches River have been spotted at least once every summer. Witnessed by thousands of people over the decades, the Ghost Riders have become one of Texas' most enduring folktales. In 1915, country singer Stan Jones immortalized them in his classic song "Ghost Riders in the Sky," and as years have gone by, the general public has largely forgotten the Riders' ugly origins. Today, the Ghost Riders are associated more with their amazing natural spectacle than their dark past.

Nevertheless, it is the curse of their evil past that has kept them coming to the Neches River year after year. Their crimson appearance against the setting sun is nothing less than an unholy condemnation, and as long as the Ghost Riders continue to appear, we know that somewhere the riders continue to pay the price for their earthly iniquities.

Stampede Mesa

The legend of Stampede Mesa takes us back to the fall of 1889, among the cottonwoods, curly mesquite and sage grass of Crosby County, Texas, where a group of cowboys was gathering an enormous herd of 1500 longhorn together after another grueling day on the trail. The cowboys guided their herd atop a mesa that was well known among local cowpunchers as an ideal spot for northward-bound cattle drives. A 200-acre plateau covered in lush grass, the mesa was bordered to the south by a sheer cliff that dropped over 100 feet into the White River below. The natural barrier allowed outfits that bedded down here to cut their night guard in half, giving the cowboys a few extra hours of sorely needed rest. The mesa-top had been used by trail crews as a resting ground for as long as herds were being driven north out of Texas.

Tired, hungry and grimy, the cowboys and their herd arrived at the mesa just as the sun was slipping below the western horizon. The end of their day in sight, the cowboys were salivating at the idea of beans, bacon and bedrolls as they rode up onto the plateau. That was before they saw the rickety old cowpuncher who was already camped there, watching over a tiny herd of 40 emaciated steers. The arriving cowboy outfit was just as thrilled about seeing this small-time rancher as he was about seeing them. The old man promptly began cursing as the approaching cattle swamped the area, turning the two separate herds into one enormous mass of cattle.

"You damn fools!" the old man roared at the approaching riders, surprising them with the gusto of his fury. "No one's resting a heartbeat 'til we cut my dogies out of that mess."

Cowboys had a difficult job: long hours, thirsty cattle and the danger of a stampede—and occasionally a good old-fashioned haunting.

The trail boss looked from the confusion of animals around them to the weary faces of his cowboys to the indignant man who was standing staring up at them with a scowl on his face and his arms akimbo. "Ain't gonna happen tonight, old-timer," the trail boss said, "me and my boys are way too beat to be sortin' out steers. We'll look after it in the mornin'. "

"Like hell you will," the old man shot back. "I ain't plannin' on getting a late start tomorrow just cause you boys can't finish your day."

By now, the entire outfit was pulled up around them—nine tired men who had been in the saddle for about four hours too long that day. "I reckon you didn't hear me right, friend," the cowboy responded again, a trace of menace in his voice. "We'll clear this mess up in the mornin'. This day o' work's over."

The solitary cowpoke was about to bark back, but he was silenced by the sound of pistol hammers cocking. Suddenly finding himself standing at the wrong end of many shooting irons, the old man swallowed his anger. "I assume we understand each other now," the trail boss said. "If there's anything else you want to say, I'm free after supper."

That ended the discussion. The old man glowered at the trail drivers as he stormed off, disappearing into the thick herd of animals as the cowboys dismounted and began setting up camp.

None of the cowboys saw the lone rancher while they were eating, and he still hadn't returned to his camp when those men not on first watch settled down in their bedrolls. Not that it really mattered to the exhausted trail drivers, who were too tired to think about where the old man was, let alone talk about him. By the time the first handful of stars appeared in the sprawling Texas sky, the outfit was a snoring circle of comatose cowboys.

That was until a dreadful rumbling sound woke them in the middle of the night. The same word flashed through the mind of each of the cowboys: stampede. They dashed for their horses as the ground shook and the enormous herd roared towards them from somewhere in the darkness. Leaping into their saddles, the trail drivers desperately tried to corral their stampeding herd. Caught unaware by the sudden rush and barely able to see in the pitch darkness, they stood next to no chance of averting the disaster that was about to transpire. Each of the cowpunchers was dreadfully aware that the cattle were stampeding south towards the 100-foot dropoff into the White River. They were all imagining the horrific scene as it played itself out just beyond their sight—hundreds upon hundreds of Texas longhorn plunged from the mesa cliff to certain death below.

The stampede had taken a terrible toll on the herd by the time it had run itself out. All but 300 cattle had fallen over the edge of the mesa; down at the base of the cliff, a gory mess of thousands of pulverized animals was draining into the White River. Among these lost steers were the bodies of two dead cowboys who had been swept over the side while trying to head off the stampeding herd. For a long while, the surviving trail drivers were only able to fester in mute shock, unable to come to terms with what had just happened. Finally, the trail boss spoke up, his voice a tense cord strung between rage and grief. "The sky is clear, and there ain't a trace of a storm on the wind. What the hell made 'em bolt?"

"Coulda been a gang of Comanche," one of the cowboys offered, "or maybe a rattler got 'em spooked."

"Wasn't no stinkin' Comanche," another cowboy said from the darkness. "Wasn't no snake, prairie dog or elephant either. I saw who did it. It was that blasted old man; I saw him wavin' a blanket and whoopin' away on the north end of the mesa. He got the cattle going before I could stop him."

"You're foolin'," the trail boss said, incredulous.

"No, I ain't. It was that old cowpuncher. I saw him. Man must be right loco to do a thing like this."

"Makes no difference to me what he is," the trail boss barked. "You ride out right now and find that vermin. Bring 'im back alive; he's gonna pay for what happened here tonight."

With that, the cowhands galloped north in pursuit of the man who was responsible for wiping out their herd and killing two of their number. The old man didn't give much of a chase; the horsemen caught up to him before he crossed the White River. Riding down on him with murder in their eyes, the cowboys promptly captured him and brought him back to their camp atop the mesa. Pleading his innocence the entire time, the old man's words fell on deaf ears.

"What you boys gonna do?" the petrified captive asked of the gathered cowboys.

"Well, I reckon we should send you after those steers you got so ornery about, old-timer," the trail boss answered. "What do you think?"

The poor man was silenced with a gag before he was able to answer. They then bound his hands behind his back and wrapped a blindfold around his head. Blindfolding his horse next, the cowboys then drove the man and his mount forward. Sightless, man and beast went forward for a few dozen feet before they hit the edge of the cliff. In another moment, they were gone, vanishing off the mesa in the dim light of the early morning.

The riders took off soon after that, taking the paltry remnant of their shattered herd with them, but the mesa they left behind would never be the same. No cattle outfit would ever again feel right staying at the once-popular resting spot.

Rumors began circulating among cattlemen in the region, stories of bizarre and inexplicable events that set cowboys and the cattle they guarded on edge. Entire herds of steers would become restless on the mesa top. More than once, cowboys resting on the mesa for the night would have to think fast when their herd, suddenly and without any apparent cause, began stampeding for the southern cliff. If not for the skill and bravery of a few cowboys, the 1889 disaster may have been repeated more than once.

No longer a desirable stopping place for trail outfits, the mesa acquired a dark reputation among Texan ranchers. They took to calling it "Stampede Mesa," a moniker for both the tendency it evoked amongst resting cattle and the unfortunate legend of its provenance. If most trail outfits avoided Stampede Mesa as a matter of practicality, few trail drivers gave the legend too much thought. One might say that the men born of the hard ranching culture of Texas tended to be not too talkative about these sorts of matters, and anyone who brought up the legend of Stampede Mesa around a bar or a campfire would likely get either laughed at or cussed out.

Nevertheless, there were cowboys whose experiences atop Stampede Mesa would make them clam up whenever members of their rough fraternity scoffed at the legend—men who experienced deeply disturbing things while riding the night guard over their herds. Some swore that they saw a glimmering apparition of a blindfolded man galloping up and down the northern line on a phantom mount and producing a bloodcurdling shriek as he went, scaring the cattle into a stampede. Other cowboys would say, when they were in company they could trust, that they saw an entire herd of ghostly cattle charging south across the mesa. Their movement made no sound, but the moment this phantom herd passed through live cattle, the living animals would suddenly surge southward along with the dead. There was good reason, then, to avoid Stampede Mesa.

The open range didn't last for too many years after 1889, and as ever fewer cattle drives made their way past the storied plateau, warnings of the strange goings-on atop the mesa were heard less and less. That isn't to say, however, that the tale of Stampede Mesa was forgotten completely. For even though traffic past the mesa subsided over the years, the phantom herd and its ghostly caretaker still haunt the 200-acre stretch of Texas upland.

Nocturnal sightings on Stampede Mesa continue to this very day. Some witnesses have corroborated the old legend, speaking of seeing the silvery form of a blindfolded old man atop a galloping horse, moving with unearthly speed across the mesa. In the past, these accounts have mostly come from Crosby County youth, often from young men driving out to the mesa at night looking for thrills—their wild cavorting cut short by the sight of the spectral rider tearing across the landscape, howling madly at the southern cliff that he was driven over so many years ago.

Others claim to have witnessed another sort of phenomenon on Stampede Mesa, this one more awe inspiring than appalling. It happens only on certain fall evenings, when the sun is low on the western horizon and the clouds are scarlet plumes and streaks across an especially dazzling western sky. It is then that an enormous herd of rushing cattle appears amongst the clouds right over Stampede Mesa. They remain visible for only a few minutes, as long as it takes them to traverse the distance of the plateau and vanish back into the clouds. And just before they disappear, the sound of a screaming man drifts in, as if heard from a great distance, like an echo on the wind.

Out of Nothing, in the Middle of Nowhere

The particulars of this folktale have been lost over the years. Forgotten are the names of the two cowboys lost on the snowswept expanse of Park County, Wyoming. No one can say for sure when and even where the event took place—only that it occurred during an especially cruel winter sometime in the last century, on a secluded stretch of ranchland. Yet the tale has been told and retold so many times—passed from person to person, generation to generation, around campfires, in books and in newspapers—that it stands as one of Wyoming's most time-tested legends, having been around nearly as long as the cowboy himself.

For the sake of the story, we'll call the two cowpunchers John and Bill. What is known about the pair is that one of them, Bill, was an older, more experienced hand, and John was a young greenhorn who had just earned his spurs. The two men were assigned as line riders on the outer borders of their ranch for the winter. In the days before barbed wire, the responsibility fell on cowpunchers to patrol the perimeters of their employers' ranches during the winter months, ensuring that no cattle strayed too far looking for shelter or pasture. It was tough work. Riding long distances between wintering stations for the duration of the season, ranch hands often had to brave raging blizzards and fierce temperatures on this extended sentry duty. For many cowboys, this border patrol was made worse by loneliness, as many ranch bosses assigned solitary patrols, condemning a few unfortunate cowboys to complete isolation for the entire season.

Luckily for John and Bill, their ranch boss wasn't so cruel. Youngster and veteran were given the patrol duty together, and for the first few months of their line-riding tenure, things went smoothly. Well, as smoothly as could be expected for such a fierce winter. It was one of the hardest seasons anyone could remember, with temperatures dipping below −30° F and snowdrifts piling up over 6 feet high. The men were hard pressed to make their rounds, often losing their way and consistently arriving at their ranch stations several hours late, frozen, tired and hungry. But few could endure deprivation and difficulty like the early American cowboy, and both John and Bill bore the harsh conditions with the mythic stoicism of their kind.

Working steadily through November and December without any incident, the pair soon found the monotony of their assignment as much of a challenge as the harsh climate. They gave up any attempts at conversation after the first month of work, and the snow-logged days quickly blended into one another, turning the days and weeks into a blurred mishmash of unpleasant sensations. Hours on the trail were marked by how numb face and fingers were; living cattle that bore their ranch's brand were herded back to where they belonged; dead cattle were skinned for their hides; wolves were shot on sight.

Everything was proceeding with mind-numbing repetition until one January morning, when Bill was woken by especially fierce winds screaming through the tiny log station he and John had bedded in the night before. "Listen to that," the old man muttered to himself, shaking off his sleep. "It must be really comin' down out there." Their quarters were so small that he didn't have to get out of bed to open the door. Reaching for the door handle, Bill gasped at the sight that greeted him when he pulled the portal open. It was the worst blizzard he had ever seen in all his days in the saddle. "Damn, what the hell are we goin' to do 'bout this?"

The sudden blast of cold air woke John. Rubbing the sleep from his eyes, the young man stared out the open door and let out a low whistle. "We got one hell of a ride ahead of us today, old-timer, make no mistake."

Bill got up to close the door, having to lean heavily against the wind to latch it shut. He lit the kerosene lamp in the tiny cabin and looked at his young companion. "I don't know if we're goin' anywhere today. Might be best to just sit tight and wait 'til it blows over. Looks mighty mean out there." These were more words than the man had spoken in the last month.

John stared doubtfully at his bearded companion. In the dim kerosene glow, he looked more grizzly bear than man. "You gotta be kiddin' me," the cowpuncher snorted his response, "stay in *this* shack for the day? I'd go stir crazy, shucks. I couldn't deal with it. Besides, ever think of what might happen if we stay put? We might just get snowed in here—it's piling up pretty quick. No offense, Bill, but I've got no desire to be buried in this box with you. I say we ride this storm out."

"I'm telling ya, kid, we won't be able to see a thing out there. We'll get lost; we'll freeze. I like our odds better sitting tight and waitin' it out. Hopefully it doesn't last more than the day. If we have to, we dig ourselves out tomorrow."

John's eyes grew a bit wild at the suggestion. It became obvious to Bill that the youngster was a bit squirrelly about small spaces. He knew with one look at the scared young man's face that staying put wouldn't be an option. "Well, I don't intend to sit here and lose my mind," John said, throwing a glance at the close walls of the shed. "When I make it back to the ranch, I'll send the boss' wife out to get you, how about that?"

Bill let out a resigned sigh. He knew it was dangerous going out, but he knew that his partner would go out by himself if that's what it came to; he couldn't let that happen. "All right then, have some jerky. We'd best get goin' quick, before the snow piles up any more."

After a quick breakfast of beef jerky and melted snow, the two strapped on their wool chaps, buttoned their coats high, pulled their hats low and waded out into the blasting snow. Making their way to the lean-to that their horses were stabled under, the pair swung into their saddles and headed out, their mounts plowing through the vicious blizzard. Less than an hour after they had left the station, they were lost.

The blizzard whitewashed the Wyoming landscape with an indiscriminating brush. The snow fell so thickly that the two cowboys couldn't even tell the sky apart from the ground; their horses' tracks vanished almost as quickly as they were formed behind them. The entire world was a frigid white void, and the two men fought back a swelling panic as they realized that they were about as lost as two people could be. "What're we gonna do?" John yelled above the blustering blizzard.

"Not much we can do but keep goin," Bill answered back through the ice-capped mess of his frozen beard. He untied his lariat and handed one end to the young cowboy. "Tie this end around your saddle," Bill hollered, "I'll keep the other end on mine. Try your best to stay close, keep moving."

John tried his best to put on a brave face. "Hell, Bill, you should see yourself right now. You look like the goddamned Wendigo." The young man's laugh sounded small and desperate in the roaring wind. Bill smiled back. Both men were terrified.

It is impossible to say how long they rode through the storm, but by all accounts, both men were well past exhaustion and coming nigh on death when their horses practically stumbled into a ramshackle wooden structure that seemed to materialize out of nowhere. Neither Bill nor John had the wherewithal to comment on the sudden appearance of this building. Both practically fell off their mounts and made their way along the building wall until they found the door; frantically digging the snow away from the entrance, Bill and John somehow managed to pry the door open wide enough to fit through.

The pair lay in the pitch darkness of the building for a long time, regaining their wits and their strength. Bill was the first to break the silence. "Jesus, Mary and Joseph, that was a close thing." John was still lying there when the cowpuncher got up to take a look around. Within a few moments, he had a kerosene lantern lit and was inspecting the place by the lamp's dim light. "John," he called out of the darkness, "do you remember anything about a saloon being built around these parts?"

The young man regained his composure and got to his feet. "Ain't no saloons around here old-timer. You know that; it's all ranchland and nothin' else for miles around. Closest gambling hall's down in Meeteetsee."

"Well, that can't be."

"And why the hell not?"

"'Cause we're in a saloon right now."

By this time, Bill had found another lantern and lit it. The room came into view under the faint kerosene light, revealing what was indeed an abandoned saloon. A motionless roulette wheel was located right next to a dusty faro table. Old paintings of half-clothed women adorned the walls, and a shelf lined with mostly empty bottles was mounted behind a bar opposite the entrance. The two single flames from the lanterns revealed chairs and playing cards strewn across the plank floor.

John whistled. "What is this place? If there was a saloon on this ranch, all of us'd know about it without a doubt. I mean this ain't possible."

"Possible or not, we're alive 'cause we had the good fortune of running into it," Bill responded. "Now let's heat this place up."

They tore apart the saloon's tables and chairs, using the wood for fuel. Before long, the two had a roaring fire going in the hearth. Roasting some frozen game they had bagged a few days previous, Bill and John devoured their dinner with the zeal of men who had come too close to their end. Only after they were done their eating did the two bother to take stock of the abandoned building.

"So what do you make of this, Bill?" the young man asked as he surveyed the derelict building. "No way there could have been a saloon built on the boss' ranch without us hearing about it." Bill took a long time to answer, listening to the angry wind moan and howl as he sat next to the fire, looking at the way the dancing shadows and flickering light made the bottles, tables and chairs come to life. Bill looked hard at the room around him, imagining the bustle of drunks and gaming men that would have once filled the establishment. Glancing over at the bar, Bill nearly jumped out of his skin at the sight of a bartender standing there, looking right at him.

"Jesus, Bill!" John yelled at his startled partner. "What's gotten into you? You lookin' at a ghost?"

Bill blinked once, and the bartender was gone. He rubbed his eyes and looked again; there was nothing there. "Eyes just playin' tricks on me," the old cowpuncher finally said. "And I don't know what to make of this bar," he responded to the youngster's earlier question. "Maybe we went farther than we thought. Hell, for all we know, we could be in Montana right now." John chuckled at the idea of having gone that far astray on their snow-packed ride.

His laughter was answered by an eerie chuckle that sounded from the opposite corner of the bar. The dry rasping chortle carried on for a few seconds before fading under the sound of the howling wind. Both men heard it, and the sound sent shivers up their spines. Instinctively, they yanked their Colts from their holsters and trained them on the unknown presence in the shadow. "Who's there?" Bill yelled out to the dark corner, cocking the hammer of his pistol. No one answered. Bill called out again, only to be answered by the same silence.

"Someone's foolin' with us in here," John hissed at Bill. "I say we jump him."

Bill nodded. "On my count."

With kerosene lantern in one hand and revolver in the other, the two men ran across the saloon towards the corner; they stopped when they were close enough to see that no one was there. John lifted his lantern and squinted hard at the deserted corner, as if something might appear if he looked hard enough.

"I swear I heard someone laughing over here," John whispered.

Bill nodded his agreement. "I heard it too." The two men stood there as the wind wailed and their hearts pounded. And then another voice came from the bar area; the voice yelled something unintelligible, sounding like the caller was hollering over a great distance. Both men reacted on the same impulse, instantly running to the bar with their gun barrels leading the way. Yet when they got to the bar, they saw that it too was deserted.

"What kind of unholy trap have we fallen into?" John asked, looking at Bill with eyes full of fear. Another voice sounded in the room, this one much closer than the call from the bar, but still unintelligible. The two men swung their lanterns in the direction of the voice; as before, there was no one there. One after another, noises began to fill the abandoned saloon. The two bewildered cowboys listened as the bar came to life. All around them, the clink of glasses, hubbub of conversation, snap of playing cards and whir of the roulette table filled the air. Backing up to the fireplace, Bill and John fed the fire until it was a roaring blaze, hoping perhaps that the light would rid the room of the phantom bustle. If anything, the more they stoked the fire, the louder the sounds got.

As scared as the two were, they both knew that certain and frigid death awaited them outside. And so with their backs against the fire, Bill and John sat there through the night, both their pistols drawn and cocked. Yet there was nothing to shoot at. Even as the din got louder, the saloon was still completely empty—its chairs unoccupied, its bottles untouched. The two men would never forget how terrified they were by the supernatural clamor, for it seemed that the livelier it got, the greater the sense of desolation in the saloon. It was as if the sounds of the once-boisterous business only accentuated its stark emptiness, as if they were trapped in a graveyard full of talking tombstones.

Neither Bill nor John believed their eyes when the sun's first rays streamed through the roof and walls. It dawned on them then that they could no longer hear the wind howling outside. The saloon had gone silent as well—still and silent as a tomb. Not that it mattered anymore; morning had arrived. The two men were out the door and running to their horses in a heartbeat, squinting in the brilliance of the sunny morning as they vaulted into their saddles. And then they were gone, plowing away from the lone building without so much as a look back.

No one can say how long it took them to make their way to the ranch, but the pair did not finish their line duties that winter, calling it quits the same morning they galloped away from the saloon. Riding into the ranch compound later on that same month, Bill and John wasted no time telling everyone in the outfit about their experience, asking each cowpuncher what they knew about this building. Yet there wasn't a man in the outfit who knew anything about it. Some of the older cowpunchers even swore that this saloon could not exist—that they had been among the first white men to arrive in the region, and no such establishment had ever been built. "Think about it," they scoffed. "Who in their right mind would open up a saloon out there when there ain't a soul around to gamble a single penny?"

Who indeed? Nevertheless, the cowboys swore on their lives that if it weren't for that saloon in the middle of nowhere, they wouldn't have lives to swear on. Over the years, the tale of the phantom saloon spread across Wyoming, becoming something of a legend among ranchers in the region. And while the two cowpunchers went to their graves swearing that their account was the truth, to this day, no one in Park County has ever laid eyes on a solitary saloon standing in the middle of nowhere. Is the story of this abandoned building a tall tale or terrifying truth? Only two long-dead cowboys and the Wyoming wind can say for sure.

3
Forts

The Ghost of Catherine Sutler

Hunger. Heat. Thirst. Indians. Monotony. Madness. The way west was fraught with difficulty for early pioneers. Whether they went along the Santa Fe Trail, Fremont's Route or the California/Oregon Trail—through short-grass prairie, sagebrush, red rock or white-capped mountains—America's first settlers dealt with all sorts of dangers and deprivations as they trudged towards their promised lands. For far too many, the paths across the unsettled territories were trails of heartache and misery, where the promises of the western horizon were matched by innumerable personal failures along the way.

The journey of the Sutler family is just one doleful yarn, a single tale of frontier tragedy among many. But for citizens of Fort Leavenworth, Kansas, the Sutler story is an account that will not die. It continues to come to life with every sighting of Catherine Sutler's sorrowful spirit as she wanders through the fort at night, looking for some sign of the children she lost over 100 years ago. Her ghost has been seen drifting among the tombstones of the National Cemetery, holding a lantern in one upraised hand, hunched over and peering into the darkness. She has been heard on the Trail West Golf Course, her voice drifting over the green, repeating the names of her two children over and over before fading into the wind. And then there are those who have gotten a closer look at Mrs. Sutler's pale phantom. Townsfolk going for late-night walks have practically run into her on Leavenworth's sidewalks, coming under the scrutiny of her vacant eyes as she searches for the faces of her missing children. Appearing countless times over the last century, Catherine Sutler is Fort

Leavenworth's most famous ghost, a skin-crawling apparition whose frequent sightings remind witnesses of the hard
history of their land.

It was the summer of 1880 when the Sutler family hitched
their wagon, packed up what they needed and rolled out of
Indiana, hoping to start a new life in the Oregon Territory.
Leaving everything they knew behind them for good, the
Sutlers must have been as frightened as they were excited,
uncertain as they were optimistic, anxious as they were
determined. But whatever hopes and dreams occupied them
as they began their journey, only in their darkest moments
would they have dared to imagine the fate that was waiting.

They arrived in Fort Leavenworth early that fall. The
famous fort on the Missouri River was the head of practically every major trail into the Great Plains, and it was
choked with covered wagons and restless homesteaders
when the Sutlers arrived. Having relatives in the fort, the
Sutlers planned on resting in Leavenworth for a few days
before hitting the California/Oregon Trail. The family didn't
know it at the time, but their great adventure west would
end at the fort.

Catastrophe came quietly to the Sutler family. It happened early in the morning on the second day they were in
Leavenworth. Hiram Sutler was doing some spot repairs on
the wagon while his wife, Catherine, was putting a breakfast
together. "Ethan! Mary!" she called out to her two children,
who emerged, groggily, from their tent. "We need firewood
for breakfast."

The two kids knew an order when they heard one and
went without a word, wiping sleep from their eyes as they
stumbled towards the west bank of the Missouri River in

search of driftwood. Catherine hadn't looked up from the meal she was preparing when she addressed her son and daughter, not knowing that these terse words would be the last she would utter to her children.

Hiram and Catherine waited for about half an hour before they went out looking for their children. They searched all along the riverbank, but there was no sign of Ethan or Mary. The couple asked everyone they ran into if they had seen their son and daughter, but no one was able to give an answer. Morning turned to midday, and neither Ethan nor Mary had turned up. By the time the sun set on that fateful day, Hiram and Catherine were desperate. They got together a search party and searched from dusk till dawn for the better part of the next week—but no trace of the kids was found. While Hiram and Catherine were both muddling through their loss, everyone else eventually took it as the sad truth that young Ethan and Mary had become two more victims of the Missouri River's dangerous waters.

It might have been said that Hiram Sutler had the hardest time of all accepting the fate of his kids, for Catherine refused to even consider the chance that her kids were gone. While Hiram was floundering in grief, Mrs. Sutler continued to hunt for the children she was sure were still alive. Day after day, she spent all her time wandering through Fort Leavenworth, the cemetery, the banks of the Missouri, the surrounding countryside, looking high and low, east and west, for any sign of her missing kids. Even as fall turned to winter and frost tipped the dying grass, Catherine continued to make her rounds. Locals grew used to the sad sight of the solitary woman walking the streets well past sunset, clutching a cloak tightly around her with one hand, holding a lantern aloft in the other, calling out the names of her children in the dark.

More than once, Hiram tried to tell his wife there was no way their kids could still be alive, but Catherine would only respond with a look that said her husband had no idea what he was talking about. "I'm telling you, Cathy," Hiram would continue, as gently as he could, "Ethan and Mary are in God's hands now."

"What in blazes are you talking about, you old fool," Catherine would reply angrily, "can't you hear them calling?"

By the time snow began to fall on Fort Leavenworth, it was largely believed that Catherine had gone mad. Walking all day and eating next to nothing, she had come to resemble a walking scarecrow, with her cloak drawn over her bony shoulders and a disturbing absence in her dark eyes. Poor Hiram, worried about his wife's health, tried everything to stop her from going out on her searches, but there was nothing he could do. He was about to request that the authorities lock her up in the local jailhouse, but the idea came too late; Catherine's body finally gave out.

Soldiers had found her near the Missouri River, lying face down in the snow. By the time they carried her back to Hiram, she had regained consciousness, but it was clear that she wouldn't be alive for much longer. Having contracted pneumonia, Catherine Sutler shook through a delirious fever for about a day and a half before she died. Hiram hitched his wagon the same day his wife expired, sickened by the horrible chasm between his family's hopes for the West and their reality. He turned his back on that horizon and drove his wagon back to Indiana, a devastated man. That spring, Hiram was in for the shock of his life. A few months after he built his new farmhouse, he was visited by a United States soldier from Fort Leavenworth, who arrived with, miracle of all miracles, his two children. It turned out that they had fallen into the Missouri River and were swept downstream for many miles. They would have surely died if a group of Fox Indians hadn't spotted them in the Missouri's current and pulled them out. The Indians waited until winter was over before they rode them back to Fort Leavenworth. Whatever joy Hiram felt at the return of his children was deadened by the fact that his wife wasn't there to share it. *She was right,* Hiram thought to himself as he wrapped his arms around Ethan and Mary, *they were still alive.*

Unfortunately, neither death nor the eventual discovery of Ethan and Mary brought an end to Catherine Sutler's tortured ramblings in and around Fort Leavenworth. First rumors of the ghost of Catherine Sutler were spread in frightened whispers among pioneers living in the area. She was seen along the banks of the Missouri River at night, frail and hunched, holding her lantern high and peering into the dark waters. "Ethan! Mary!" came her hollow cries, which carried over the river and through the fort, bringing chills to all who heard her.

As time passed, more and more people had run-ins with Catherine's pale apparition. Dressed in the same garments she wore while alive, Catherine would have appeared just as she had when she was living if it weren't for the startling pallor of her face and hands. She'd always been pale, but those who saw her ghost claimed that her skin was so white it gave off a faint glow. And there were her eyes—while it was said that her madness was apparent during the final days of her life, those luckless men and women who looked upon her now were stricken by the frightening nothingness in her eyes. No one who saw her was the same again.

Over the years, there were far too many Kansans who could make that claim. Catherine's ghost did not stop appearing when her children were reunited with their father. She continued to haunt the northeastern corner of Kansas years later, after Hiram had passed on, and she continued her search for her children even after both of them had grown old and died. Indeed, Catherine Sutler is still seen by residents of Fort Leavenworth today, her anachronous visage drifting through the well-lit streets of the historic military base. She is still heard calling out for Ethan and Mary. It seems likely that the phantom frontier woman will never give up her fruitless search, making her sad tale one of the most enduring pioneer ghost stories of the West.

The Ghost of Elizabeth Polly

Sarah Jasper was in her car on a summer night in 1995, driving nowhere in particular, the headlights of her Toyota Corolla small in the immense blackness of the surrounding plains. Sarah was a recent nursing graduate who had just started working in Hays, Kansas, as an emergency room nurse. Having studied at a Canadian university, she was new in town and didn't know too many people, so she spent many of her nights driving through the surrounding countryside, letting the hum of her tires over the highway and the vast Kansan night calm her. Events on this night, however, would be far from tranquil.

The apparition appeared on a back road when Sarah was just south of Hays. It came out of nowhere—a woman in a blue dress crossing the road, illuminated by Sarah's head-lights for an instant before the Corolla flew into her. In one horrific moment, Sarah took note of the lacework on the woman's bonnet just as the grill of the car passed through the apparition. Sarah would later recall that there was no jolt of impact, that it was as though the car passed straight through nothing at all, but at the time, the young nurse reacted quickly. Telling herself to ignore her pounding heart, she slammed on the brakes, hit the hazard lights and ran out onto the road. But where the bonneted woman should have been was only a deserted road. Sarah was alone in the blus-tering wind of the Kansas night.

She did not know it at the time, but Sarah had just had an encounter with one of Hays' most enduring spirits: the "Blue Light Lady," a legendary ghost dating back to the town's ear-liest years, when Fort Hays was a wild and wooly military base in Sioux territory. People knew her when she was alive as Elizabeth Polly, a hard and humble frontier woman whose actions during an 1867 cholera epidemic in Fort Hays turned her into one of the West's folk heroes.

She and her husband, Ephraim, had been in town for only a few months when the epidemic hit Hays, but Elizabeth quickly took the matter personally when men began to die. Dubbed the "Angel of the Plains," Elizabeth worked tirelessly among the afflicted soldiers, providing care and comfort to the mortally ill men in the fort. Pretty well all her waking hours were spent tending to the sick, but whenever she got any time to herself, Elizabeth would light to the hills south of Hays, where she would look west as the sun set. It was during these serene moments that Elizabeth fell in love with the wild land—when the enormous crimson-streaked sky colored the short-grass prairie in shades of red, and the blowing wind washed the death of the day off her. It was then that she was at peace.

Many chroniclers have written that Elizabeth knew her death was imminent. "When my time comes, Ephraim," she would say to her husband when they were alone, "bury me atop the south hill."

To the dismay of all, Elizabeth's premonition came true. She contracted cholera before the year was over and was on her deathbed soon after that. The whole fort mourned the demise of Elizabeth Polly; rough soldiers would lower their voices when they spoke of the sick young woman dying within their walls. Men more inclined to brawling and boozing bowed their heads and doffed their caps when they went in to visit their ailing angel of the plains.

And then one day, her light went out. There was a somber mood in Hays and throughout the surrounding plains as the funeral procession marched out to her favorite lookout point south of the fort. They tried to bury her on the hilltop but found that the ground was too rocky for a suitable grave. So they interred Elizabeth Polly at the base of the hill instead, planting a wooden headstone at her gravesite. The exact location of her remains, however, has become something of a Hays mystery. Years after she was buried, a prairie fire blazed over the hill, completely incinerating her tombstone.

Although her remains are lost, her legacy has remained in the local chronicle. A park on Hays' Schmaller Avenue was named after the town's first spark of civility, and in 1968 a monument for Elizabeth Polly was erected atop Sentinel Hill, the promontory she loved so much when she was alive. And despite her absence from any formal historical record,

Elizabeth Polly's story has been passed through the generations, becoming one of the area's prominent folktales. Of course, the fact that the ghost of Elizabeth Polly is believed to wander the area has done much to keep her alive in the minds of Kansans.

Bob Wilhelm, director of the Fort Hays Museum, considers the story of Elizabeth Polly's ghost to be an undeniable part of Hays' history. "It was in the 1890s when Elizabeth's ghost first appeared in print. The story about two guys working on top of Sentinel Hill appeared in a local paper. They were just finishing up their labors when they saw a dark-haired woman walk along the top of the hill. She walked along for a few yards before vanishing right in front of them."

Over the years, her apparition has appeared time and again. The description is always the same: an austere-looking woman with dark hair, a long dress and a bonnet tied tightly around her head. Locals began referring to her as the Blue Light Lady because of the blue light seen shimmering around her. While she has often been spotted atop Sentinel Hill, many have seen her anywhere between her lookout point and the town of Hays. Farmers working their fields late have stared wonderstruck at the sight of the blue-lit woman gliding over their crops. Couples looking for seclusion have been startled out of their courting when the glimmering woman in the anachronistic dress drifts by them. More than one motorist driving south of Hays at night has seen her moving along the side of the road. Some, like young Sarah Jasper, have been scared half to death believing that they struck a living woman.

Elizabeth Polly seldom appears for long. Witnesses claim that she is visible for only a couple of minutes at most. It is said that the sight of her always causes a distinct feeling of fear and unease that far outlasts the few moments she appears. When she vanishes, she always vanishes suddenly, leaving no trace of her passing.

No one can say for sure why Elizabeth Polly's spirit continues to haunt the area. There are all the obvious guesses. Some say that the compassionate young woman was so attached to Sentinel Hill that she hasn't been able to leave it behind in death. Others have stated that her spirit is unsettled because her body wasn't buried atop Sentinel Hill as she requested. Another guess is that the ghost of the dutiful nurse is convinced that there are still cholera-stricken men in Hays, and it continues to make the trip into town hoping to help.

Whatever the case, Elizabeth Polly's ghost has appeared with such regularity over the years that she may be considered Hays' oldest resident. Certainly, her tale has become woven into the history of the Kansan town. "There are some people who think the legend of Elizabeth Polly is silly," Bob Wilhelm says, "but it's been around for so long that she really has become part of this town. We can't deny the legacy of this brave young woman on the plains."

The Alamo

*No book on the Old West would be complete without
a story of the Alamo. Here, reproduced from my
Ghost Stories of America, is a story of this
important—and ghostly—landmark.*

The Alamo. It is one of America's premier historical land-
marks. Built by Franciscan monks in 1718, the monastery
was converted into an altar of American democracy on
March 6, 1836, when General Antonio Lopez de Santa Anna
gave the order that sent 4000 Mexican soldiers charging
towards the near 200 Texan men garrisoned inside. Almost
everyone knows the outcome of the frantic hour-and-a-half
battle, where all but a handful of Texans were killed in the
most publicized last stand in military history. Since that dramatic battle of the Texas Revolution, "Remember the Alamo!"
has become a rallying cry for beleaguered American troops
wherever they might be, bolstering soldiers' courage in the
heat of battle. And so the spirit of the Alamo continues to
live on, occupying an important place in the mythos of a
dauntless American democracy, resolved to remain vigilant
in the face of any enemy before it.

Yet as many San Antonio residents know, the spirit of the
Alamo lives on in more ways than one; the fort is deemed
one of the most haunted sites in the state of Texas. Perhaps it
is the historical significance of the Texans' sacrifice in the old
Franciscan monastery. The men who fell in the fort, their
deaths imbued with a timeless significance for the entire
nation, have taken on an aspect of timelessness themselves,
continuing to haunt the hallowed ground where they gave

The Alamo, in San Antonio, Texas, c. 1860 (above), may be the most haunted place in the state of Texas.

their lives for an independent Texas and an American ideal. Or it may be the sheer horror of so many individuals' final moments, where the defenders saw imminent death arriving on dark wings by crashing cannon, whistling musket ball and glinting bayonet—no quarter asked, none given. It could be that the merciless fighting that March 6 morning more than 160 years ago was so vicious that some residue of the combatants might remain behind, unable to come to terms with the brutality of their final end.

The front gates of the legendary Alamo

Either way, things have never been the same at the Alamo since the 1836 battle. Strange happenings began occurring there soon after the legendary stand. It was April 21, 1836, not a month and a half later, when Santa Anna surrendered to the Texans after a decisive defeat at the Battle of San Jacinto. Before he submitted, Santa Anna gave the Mexican garrison in San Antonio orders to destroy the Alamo's chapel, a final strike against his Texan enemies before he retreated south past the Rio Grande. But the soldiers that were sent out to destroy the occupied building were never able to carry out the command.

According to legend, the contingent of Mexicans ordered to raze the Alamo was stopped at the entrance by a terrifying sight. Six ghostly, semi-transparent soldiers stood in a half circle before the chapel door, each holding a flaming saber aloft. It was evening, and a hot orange light from the phantoms' upraised weapons flickered over the bizarre scene. The only way into the building for the Mexicans was through the six figures that were standing in their way, but not a man among them was able to take a single step towards the fort, so terrified were they of the defiant apparitions. There is no historical record of who these spirits were. It was too dark, and they were encased in too much shadow for anyone to make out any discernable features. The soldiers stood before the phantoms for a few long minutes, before the resolve of one of the Mexicans finally broke. Telling his shaking comrades they could fight "*les diablos*" if they wished, he turned his back to the Alamo and headed to his barracks. The rest of the men weren't far behind him.

This story was only the first to come out of the fort. Soon after, people started taking notice of a solitary figure that appeared atop the Alamo on some nights, moving from east to west on the south side of the roof. Some described the figure as a lone sentry, deliberately making his rounds over an anachronistic post. Others swear that there is a desperate cadence to the figure's movements, as if it is frantically looking for some sort of escape. Whatever the case, those who have actually gone on to the roof to investigate have never gotten a chance to inquire what the mysterious individual might be up to, for no one has ever seen him face to face. San Antonio used the Alamo as police headquarters through the 1890s, during which time countless officers heard the footsteps making their way across the roof of the building. Time and again, officers climbed up to see who was walking around on the roof, but there was never anyone there. After countless visitations by this mysterious rooftop interloper, policemen blamed the weather, explaining the footsteps away by surmising that they could be rain or falling objects blown in by the wind. While no one really believed these rationalizations, they helped to ease the officers' minds a little. The solitary figure atop the Alamo continues to be spotted today by San Antonio tourists and residents alike, a lone man continuing his timeless walk across the roof, motivated by a force that may forever remain a mystery.

This nocturnal figure isn't the only remnant of the 19th century that continues to haunt the Alamo. Another legend concerns a small fortune that is said to be buried in the wall of the southwest corner of the fort. According to this account, the Alamo's defenders placed all their personal treasures in one of the Alamo's bells just before the siege began and buried the bell under the fort. Many mediums who have claimed to communicate with the spirits of the dead Texans in the fort have confirmed this story. And according to some, it is no paltry treasure. One psychic has stated that over $540,000 in gold is hidden beneath the fort.

Yet unless the state of Texas is willing to take a wrecking ball to the historical site, the existence of this treasure must remain in question, a legend, rather than a fact, along with all the other supernatural tales regarding the celebrated building.

Visitors today continue to experience disturbing events at the Alamo. There are many accounts of sudden cold spots in the long barracks building, where the fiercest fighting was said to have been. Lone tourists have also heard harsh whispers hissing at them from empty space. And then there are those who have heard the brisk tramp of numerous marching feet, of painful moans carried on the ether, coming from everywhere and nowhere.

Such experiences, and all stories associated with them, are usually pigeonholed as folklore or supernatural phenomena, largely disassociated from the formal history of the fort. Nevertheless, they have proven the test of time, and over 150 years after the first supernatural experience was reported in the fort, ghost stories still abound, making the historic Alamo one of the most haunted buildings in San Antonio, if not the entire state of Texas.

4

Inns
Houses
Hotels

The Brantley Mansion

During a time when life in the West was, for the most part, brutish, precarious and short, Judge Theodore Brantley was a man who worked tirelessly for civility, community and stability. When most of the country west of the 100th meridian was populated by tribes of Indians and the young men who made war against them, Brantley built a mansion on a hill and moved there with his wife and children. When the West was wild, Judge Theodore Brantley introduced the virtues of discipline and grace.

Not that Theodore Brantley was given to excessive pontificating. In fact, the Montana Supreme Court judge was known more for his terse manner and extreme reserve than he was for any grand moralizing. The judge was a lead-by-example type of man, and everything about him, from the clothes he wore, to the way he organized each and every hour of his day, bore the mark of the civilized man at his best. He was a hard-working churchgoer who opened the door for women and consistently did all he could to see that justice was done. It was the arrival of men like Judge Theodore Brantley in the West that ushered in the beginning of the end for the region's wilder days.

Brantley's mansion was built on a hill overlooking Helena, Montana, in 1887. The house itself was a bold statement against its feral surroundings. An opulent Victorian structure that would have looked more in place on a British aristocrat's estate, the Brantley House was a veritable castle compared to many of the humble log cabins and pine plank boxes that dominated the young town of Helena. Not that there weren't other mansions in Helena; a number of residents had made

Judge Brantley built his mansion in Helena, Montana, and resided there during life and after death.

their fortunes digging gold out of the Last Chance Gulch. As might be expected of a town that grew up around a gold strike, there was no shortage of millionaires living in the frontier burg.

Nevertheless, something was different about Theodore Brantley. Maybe it was the deliberate poise of his walk as he made his way through the streets of Helena in his tailored suit and stovepipe hat. Or it could have been the manner in which he addressed every man and woman he met, with a formal courtesy that seemed out of place in the rough town. Or even yet, maybe it was his legendary work ethic; spending almost every waking hour poring over case papers and legal documents, Judge Brantley was a living example of restraint and discipline in the largely unbridled and physical world of the western frontier.

If Judge Brantley embodied the order that was coming to the Wild West, then his home was an example of every sort of luxury this civilization could provide. An enormous three-story mansion embellished with an oak interior and all the amenities that a person of the Supreme Court judge's stature would need to entertain guests, the Brantley House was more than a home. It was also a commitment to the town of Helena and the state of Montana. Judge Brantley wanted to make sure people understood that he, his wife and his three children were there to stay—that civilization had arrived in Helena. And indeed it had.

By the time Theodore Brantley died in 1922, Helena had grown past its humble provenance to become the established capital of the vigorously growing state of Montana. Time marched on, and the mansion remained in the possession of the Brantley family for nearly five decades after its original patriarch had died. Helena went through many changes, and old Judge Brantley had pretty well been forgotten by all, a minor historical figure in the vast drama of the American West. Until, that is, 1970, when the Brantley family finally sold the old house on Holter Street.

It was then, when the new owners started renovating the house, that the name "Theodore Brantley" began to be mentioned again. The first inexplicable event in the Brantley

House occurred within the first few weeks after the new family moved in. The new owners were busy gutting the third floor when they were stopped by the sound of the big front door creaking open and then slamming shut. In another moment, they could hear heavy footsteps making their way up the house's ornate spiral staircase. The footfalls were slow and loud, as if a tired man with heavy boots was being careful to take his time as he made the ascent. When the footsteps got to the third floor, they made their way down the hallway, where they stopped for a few moments at every door, opening them and then carrying on to the next. After the mysterious visitor reached the end of the hallway, the footsteps stopped.

The couple ran out to see who their guest was, but there was no one in sight. Unable to accept that a person could vanish into thin air, they conducted a thorough search throughout the entire house, yet there was nothing or no one there. Besides their three children and themselves, Brantley House was empty.

That wasn't the last time they would hear the footsteps. The invisible visitor always came during weeknights, arriving sometime past 10. He opened the front door and made his way up the spiral staircase. When he got to the third floor, he would walk down the hallway, his slow steps pausing at each door, and he would open each door slowly; the footsteps fell silent only when they got to the end of the hall.

None of the new residents would ever get a glimpse of who, or what, was coming into their home nightly, yet surprisingly enough, none of them felt threatened. Whatever these disembodied footsteps were about, the family knew that there was no intent to harm. If anything, there was a sense that something was checking up on them out of some sort of concern. They would soon discover how right they were. It turned out that the house's original patriarch, Judge Theodore Brantley, spent most of his weekdays working in his office late. His routine was dependable. Making his way up the spiral staircase after everyone was in bed, the judge would stop at each of his children's bedrooms, open the door and look in just to assure himself that everything was okay. As strange as the explanation for the disembodied footsteps was, it was the only one the new owners had, and they came to accept the presence of the concerned judge.

By all accounts, this phenomenon had not occurred in the over 80 years that the Brantley family owned the house. When the story became public, some speculated that the renovations on the third floor were somehow responsible, that the judge's spirit was woken when the rooms he had known while alive came under hammer and nail. Others pointed out that, just like Theodore Brantley's family, the new residents were a married couple with three children. It was offered that this similarity might have roused the previously latent ghost to a higher state of activity.

Whatever the case, once woken, the ghost of the Supreme Court judge did not seem too eager to fall back into oblivion. After a few weeks of the footsteps up the staircase and down the third-floor hall, the judge began wandering into the attic as well. They heard him late at night: his heavy footsteps pacing across the garret right above the master bedroom. Slow and deliberate on the creaking wood planks, the footfalls would continue back and forth until someone went up to investigate. For a while, the residents didn't know what to do about the judge's new habit, which would often keep them up for hours. That was before the married couple discovered the secret staircase hidden behind a false wall in their bedroom. The only way to the attic, the staircase was the key to stopping the footfalls on the top floor—the moment anyone stepped on the first stair, the footfalls would stop.

The Brantley family's history could explain the footsteps in the attic as well. It was said that Theodore Brantley had used the attic as a study while he was a Supreme Court judge. According to the family account, he spent many late nights there, working until the small hours of the morning. Though less was said of his poor wife, she must surely have been wakened by the sounds of his incessant pacing. The new residents sleeping in the master bedroom could attest to how distracting this habit must have been.

While the above phenomena found their explanations in Theodore Brantley's earthly habits, some aspects of the respected judge's personality would probably have been lost to history if not for the habits of the Brantley House haunt. For one, the new owners discovered that Judge Theodore Brantley was in possession of a virulent sweet tooth. The basement tenant was the first person to learn about the former owner's dietary penchant, when sweets he left out in a candy bowl started disappearing. Usually noticing the diminished bowl in the morning, the tenant took to replacing them before he headed out to work. At first, only modest quantities of M&Ms and Smarties would vanish from the bowl, but before long, the tenant found himself refilling half the bowl every day. Residents in the Brantley House just assumed that this nocturnal pilferer was one and the same as the spirit stomping around on the top floors, but what a non-physical entity would want with candy was something they could never figure out. Did the spirit of Theodore Brantley have some supernatural way of consuming these stolen treats? Or was he just moving them some place else, perhaps hiding the stolen sweets in some dark corner of the house?

The 19th-century judge's interests were not limited to 20th-century confections. He also exhibited a fascination with new technology, particularly the television and the radio. The residents came home more than once to find every television and radio in the house turned on at full volume. As disquieting as this phenomenon initially was, the Brantley House inhabitants soon got used to it, as they did all the other bizarre goings-on in the house. Turning off every blaring television and radio in the house as they scolded the judge over the cacophony of competing noises became something of a routine for the house's residents, a routine that continued until the house was sold again.

The house's current inhabitants knew about the haunting when they purchased it, and they were given a sample of what the judge's ghost was capable of the first day they were there. Taking a breather after hauling in a load of boxes, the new owners were sitting in the living room when one of their plants suddenly rose into the air, hovering about 5 feet off the floor. They just watched, shocked, as the plant floated to the middle of the room, where it hovered for a few seconds longer before falling to the ground, breaking into a mess of shattered pottery and soil.

An ominous thing to happen to anyone moving into a recently purchased home, the incident might have weighed much heavier on the minds of the new owners if the vacuum cleaner hadn't suddenly come to life then, cleaning up the mess that the old judge had just made. The current inhabitants wouldn't be subjected to any such destructive acts again, because old Judge Brantley settled into his usual supernatural routine of stomping around the house late at night, stealing unattended sweets and turning on televisions and radios.

Perhaps the judge's uncharacteristically malicious display was just a way to inform his new housemates that he was a very real presence, in spite of his incorporeal form. Or maybe he was simply protesting the previous owners' departure. Could he have been offended that they left without saying good-bye? Or it might have been frustration at his lack of say as to who he was living with; as soon as he had gotten used to one family, another replaced them. Either way, Judge Theodore Brantley has gotten used to his new housemates and hasn't broken anything since the day they arrived, his supernatural activities again consistent with the pacific personality he was once famous for.

The Ghost of Eilley Bowers

Alison "Eilley" Oram was *the* Grande Dame of early Nevada. An early settler in the Washoe Valley, she was one of the extraordinary women of western America, winning and losing her fortune by the tumultuous boom and bust conditions of the mining frontier. Born in Scotland on September 6, 1826, Eilley married when she was 15 and moved to Great Salt Lake soon after with Stephen Hunter, her devoutly Mormon husband. It would be the last time she rode on the coattails of any man.

In a time when divorce was not a realistic option for so many women, young Eilley left her husband soon after they arrived in America; the reasons behind this separation are forgotten by history, but whatever they were, they did not spoil the idea of marriage for the Scot. She married another Mormon named Alexander Cowan in 1853. Two years later, man and wife moved to what is now Nevada. Acting as Mormon missionaries, the two set up a ranch near present day Genoa, moving on to the Washoe Valley in western Nevada about one year later. While Eilley was already an anomaly among women in her willingness to settle on the rough fringes of American civilization, she became one of the legendary figures of the region when she decided to stay behind in the Washoe Valley after her husband was called back to Utah by the Mormon order.

Effectively ending her marriage to Alexander Cowan, it was not long before she was rewarded for her bold independence. Moving south to a small mining camp called Johntown, she set up a boarding house, supplying miners with decent rooms in a rough settlement where tents were the common shelter. The move was fortuitous. In 1859, gold was discovered on a nearby hill, and miners swamped into the region, bringing a suddenly booming business to the enterprising young woman. She was not content to live off the earnings of the miners, however, and soon got involved in mining herself. Living in the region before the rush of miners began, Eilley had her pick of the mining plots along Gold Hill. One of her claims bordered on another claim owned by one Lemuel "Sandy" Bowers. The handsome young Scotsman developed a deep admiration for Eilley's dauntless ambition, and the two were wed under fortunate auspices because both their claims began churning out incredible amounts of wealth.

Eilley and Sandy Bowers became Nevada's first two millionaires. Tapping into the enormous Comstock Lode, the couple became the recipients of more money than they had ever dared to imagine. This abundance of cash greased the wheels of their nuptial arrangements, and a true and lasting love formed between them. But with greater wealth came greater potential for tragedy: the more one has, the more one has to lose. Fortune's pattern of generous bestowal and cruel deprivation did not spare the Bowers. The twists of fate Eilley would suffer throughout the rest of her days turned her attention to mystical forces, and she spent the last years of her life engrossed in the spirit world, looking to the denizens of the underworld for guidance—until she became one of those spirits herself.

The Bowers' impending misfortunes arrived along with their first two children, who both died in their infancy. Perhaps the Bowers were seeking some respite from the sorrow of these losses when they commissioned their mansion to be built and took off on a 10-month trip through Europe. They came back to their newly constructed mansion along with a child whom they had adopted somewhere in the Scottish highlands; Eilley was never forthcoming about the girl's background.

But the Bowers would not have too much time to enjoy any familial happiness. Soon after they returned, their mines began to run out. Outstanding debts suddenly loomed large before the Bower family, and their savings and income rapidly deteriorated. By the time Sandy went to their mines on Gold Hill to oversee the operation, the ore had all but run out. Poverty, however, was not an issue Mr. Bower had to contend with for too long. With a broken heart and lungs full of rock dust, Sandy died of silicosis early in 1868.

Eilley was alone again, doing everything she could to raise her adopted daughter in a world that was decidedly hostile to independent women. She turned her mansion into a boarding house in hopes of paying off her debts, but her efforts were in vain. She became more removed from reality as her fortunes plummeted, yet it was in 1874, when her daughter died after her appendix burst in a Reno boarding school, that Eilley's worldview changed dramatically.

She lost her mansion in a public auction in 1876 and spent the rest of her life dabbling in the spirit world, making a meager living looking into her crystal ball, giving superstitious clients a look into their futures for a small price. She also claimed she could communicate with spirits of the departed and charged to deliver messages to clients' deceased loved ones. Spending the rest of her days wandering between California and Nevada, the once incredibly wealthy mine proprietor spent her last days in an Oakland, California, poorhouse. She died on October 27, 1903.

But that would not be the last the world would hear of Eilley Bowers. Strange things began to happen in the Bowers Mansion soon after she passed away. There were reports of mysterious sounds coming from deserted hallways and rooms. People described them as shuffling sounds; objects were being moved about, as if someone was looking for a missing possession, emptying closets, nightstands and dressers. But investigations never revealed any intruder, just an empty, rearranged chamber.

Other people claimed to see a stately looking matriarch dressed in Victorian splendor standing stoically before one of the mansion's windows, looking out on the estate's sprawling grounds. The woman was described as broad, with short dark hair and hard features, descriptions that match the portraits of the same legendary entrepreneur who had the mansion built.

These sightings have increased dramatically since the Bower Mansion was opened for tours. Many believe Eilley is returning for her crystal ball, which is displayed in the mansion today. Others think that her spirit is reliving those few days of happiness when she was living in the mansion with her daughter and husband, before the cruel hands of fate tore their household apart.

The Cain House

It might require a stretch of the imagination to see it now, but at one time, the town of Bodie, California, was the liveliest place on the eastern slope of the Sierra Nevada—or maybe "deadliest" might be a better word. The first men to arrive in the area were gold miners who had gotten wind of Waterman S. Body's modest gold strike just north of Mono Lake, near the Nevada-California border in 1859. A year later, only about 20 miners lived in the region, 20 men driven by ambition or insanity who came to live among the freezing peaks of the high Sierras in hopes of striking gold. Within two decades, this pitiful rock-scrabbling operation became the great golden Golconda of the West, and the handful of shacks and tents that housed the original prospectors were transformed into the tremendous and terrible town of Bodie.

It has been said that of the over 10,000 frontier adventurers who choked Bodie's streets in 1880, there might have

The J.S. Cain House in Bodie, California, might be home to the tortured spirit of a maid who committed suicide there.

been a dozen or so decent personalities. But for the rest of them, greed, treachery and mutual enmity was the rule. The roaring burg attracted the worst of that caste of dissolute denizens who were found in the Dodges, Tombstones and Abilenes of the country—the gunfighters, gamblers, prostitutes and con men who made the Wild West what it was. And while Bodie's gold rush lasted for less than a decade, the madness and mayhem that was planted there during those few short years can still be felt today.

Not that that there are any outlaws remaining in Bodie at this time. One of the country's best preserved ghost towns, Bodie has been made into a state historic park that draws in

The unhappy spirit has slammed doors, caused household temperatures to drop and scared people out of deep sleeps.

thousands of tourists a year. While the real town was hastily vacated after the gold ran out and fires destroyed most of Bodie's buildings, the ghost town's dramatic history has assured that it will never be forgotten, and it continues to be a popular destination for curiosity seekers, western enthusiasts and those who have a penchant for the supernatural. Indeed, many visitors to the abandoned burg have had experiences that suggest that history isn't quite done with Bodie.

Countless occurrences, strange and inexplicable, have been reported in Bodie over the years. Park employees and visitors alike have seen lights flash on and off in long-deserted buildings; mysterious apparitions have been spotted drifting across the town's graveyard around nightfall; the sounds of distant music and boisterous conversation have often been heard within a few Bodie households; and people passing by the Standard Mine shaft have sworn to have heard chains rattling and men grunting within.

But of all the strange things that have occurred in the ghost town, none is more talked about than the spirit in the Cain House. Constructed in 1873, the quaint little building was home to J.S. Cain, one of Bodie's first settlers. According to legend, Cain was one of the wealthier residents in Bodie, having made a tidy sum off land speculation in and around town, purchasing most of his real estate just before the gold rush began. Able to afford luxuries most men in Bodie could only dream about, Cain built his home, moved his wife into it and hired a Chinese maid to look after the mess. In a time when there were precious few women in the West, a man with a wife was enviable enough, but someone privileged enough to keep *two* women was a rare thing indeed.

So it was that J.S. Cain's living arrangement was the subject of a good deal of town gossip. After slogging away their days in the mineshafts, bitter miners would spend a little too much of their leisure time speculating on the sorts of things that went on in the "Cain Harem" as they threw back shots of whiskey. Bodie residents tittered and clucked whenever they walked past Cain's house, shouting jokes and obscenities at the walls and windows. This attention wasn't lost on Cain's wife, Ella, who quickly grew to resent the presence of the household maid. It didn't help that the maid was an exceedingly beautiful woman, who got just a little too much notice from Ella's husband. Ella soon became bent on ending the woman's tenure at her house.

Cain was able to hold off his wife for a short while, but it wasn't long before he realized that he would have to let the maid go. The problem was that the Chinese woman spoke next to no English, and while she understood enough to know that Cain was firing her, she couldn't comprehend why. For Cain's part, he could never have known how much the job meant to her. Perhaps she was sending her wages back to a family that was desperately in need of them in China, or maybe she was so frightened by her foreign surroundings that she couldn't comprehend life without the security of the Cain household. Whatever the case, the poor young woman was devastated. She hanged herself in her bedroom on her last night in the Cain House.

While there are no accounts of strange happenings in the house immediately after the maid killed herself, there is reason to believe that her tortured spirit lingered on there after she took her life. In recent years, the Cain House has been used as sleeping quarters for rangers working in Bodie Historic Park. It is the experiences of park employees quartering in the Cain House that have kept the legend of the Chinese maid alive. Some have woken from fitful sleeps to see a beautiful Chinese woman standing at the foot of their bed, staring at them with an unforgettable look of both fierce loathing and inexpressible sorrow. By the time these frightened witnesses sit up in alarm, the woman has vanished, leading many who have heard this story to offer that these rangers may have been dreaming. This might very well have been the case, if it weren't for the vividness of the vision, the fear pounding through witnesses' hearts and the image's continued appearance over the years.

Those visions say nothing of the other things that have occurred in the Cain House. Some haven't *seen* the Chinese maid so much as they've *felt* her, waking up to a horrifying suffocating sensation, as if a force was somehow physically constricting their lungs. Those who try to get up find their limbs pinned to their bed. The experience never lasts for more than several seconds, not long enough to cause any lasting harm, but enough to convince employees who have experienced it to never sleep in the house again. When she isn't suffocating park employees, the unhappy spirit has also been known to swing doors open and slam them shut, turn lights on and off and cause temperatures in the house to plummet. Her presence is always marked by the same strong sense of foreboding. No one who has had any experience with the Cain House's maid is too eager to go back.

Of course, the Cain House is only one story among many in Bodie, California. Many have contended that the entire town is haunted. Psychically sensitive visitors sense it through the whole ghost town—a vague yet powerful energy from the past that fills the town with an intangible air of antiquity that exceeds the real age of the ghost town.

This sensation has probably done the most to feed the legend of the curse of Bodie in the popular mind. Since the ghost town was made into a historic site, park policy has deemed that visitors aren't permitted to take anything from the ghost town; by law, not a pebble, button or splinter of wood can be touched. Yet those who have defied this regulation, and made away with a small keepsake to remember

Bodie by, are never happy with their souvenirs. More often than not, these mementos bear a strange weight with people who have taken them. Sometimes it is said that individuals with pieces of Bodie in their possession come under a streak of bad luck in their lives, losing loved ones or suffering financial difficulty or personal injury. Virulent fits of insomnia, lagging energy and bad mood swings have also been attributed to relics from Bodie. Yet the curse is not said to be permanent, for those who return their stolen items to the park are said to be instantly liberated from the grip of the ghost town.

It is a curse that has been taken very seriously—over the years, thousands of minute items taken from the park grounds have been mailed back to Bodie in unmarked packages. Apparently, the ghosts of the old boomtown are interesting to visit, but no one wants to live with them.

The Ghost of Seth Bullock

In the spring of 1876, nothing too delicate, refined or precious lived long in Deadwood. An illegal settlement in hostile Sioux Territory, Deadwood was populated by roughly 5000 of the frontier's worst men, who flocked to the area in 1875, soon after gold was discovered in the Black Hills. The cry of "Gold!" in the Dakota Territory drew in every desperate drifter from the Rio Grande to the upper Missouri. The mining camp was chock-full of gold diggers, gamblers and bad men, a murderous fraternity of mostly young males who would gladly sell their own livers—or better yet the livers of the man next to them—for a flash in the pan. During daylight hours, they teemed over the surrounding hills, digging desperately for the shining metal they coveted more than life; after the sun went down, most of them retreated into the ramshackle collection of fetid tents scattered across the bottom of Deadwood Gulch, where they would spend the night making their unique brand of hell.

During the first months of its existence, most of Deadwood's gambling houses and saloons were nothing more than huge tents where enterprising men set up crude tables and doled out shots of rotgut whiskey for inflated prices. But development came quickly to this mining community, and by 1876, most of Deadwood's business establishments were false-fronted wooden buildings lined up along broad dirt boulevards. Yet while conditions in Deadwood improved, the behavior of its dissolute citizens largely remained the same.

Life was cheap in the rough and tumble mining town. Most of the men who lived there were possessed by a virulent gold fever, which relegated every other sense and sensibility to the periphery. Deadwood's saloons became dens of homicidal jealousy and bitter intemperance; men would come to drink, mull and mutter over the gold and grievances of the day. Whiskey, frustration and firearms made for a volatile mixture, and liquor-soaked gunfights became an all-too-frequent form of expression in the lawless town. Things got worse and worse, until the legendary gunfighter, Wild Bill Hickok was shot through the back of the head while he was playing cards at the Saloon #10. That was when Seth Bullock stepped onto the scene.

He was Deadwood's first sheriff, a man who possessed such a stern, authoritarian mien that he was often mistaken for an Earp brother. The sort of man who was able to bring violent men to reason with a single glance, Seth Bullock was a natural leader among the men of the West who were inclined to take too many liberties in the lawless conditions of the frontier. One could say that Seth was born into his role as western peacemaker, having spent most of his boyhood railing against the stifling order of his father, a retired officer in the British military. And while much of his youth was passed resisting such stern parental control, when he rode out West in 1867—an ambitious 18-year-old hoping to make his fortune in the Montana Territory—he took the authority of his father with him. It shone from behind his flashing eyes, an informal, unspoken edict that practically every man in the West understood with a glance.

Distinguishing himself as a man of the law in Montana throughout the late 1860s and early 1870s, he had already served as a member of the Territorial Senate and a county sheriff by the time he followed the gold rush to Deadwood in 1876. Upon arriving in Deadwood, the first thing Seth

Seth Bullock's hotel eventually fell into disuse until renovations awakened its former glamor—along with the spirit of its first proprietor.

became aware of was a need for order. Sending his bride and their daughter to their Michigan home, he promptly went about the business of shaping up the chaotic community. After he was appointed sheriff, it did not take long. Becoming the unbending father to every badman in Deadwood, Seth and his cadre of armed deputies brought law to the Black

The legendary Seth Bullock (left) with President Theodore Roosevelt

Hills. Peace was made in the turbulent town of Deadwood with nearly no shots fired.

With law came respectability, and Seth Bullock became known across the western states as one of the premier agents of civilization. The energetic Bullock took advantage of his reputation. He built up one business after another, opening a hardware shop and hotel in Deadwood and a ranch along the Belle Fourche River, all the while dedicating time to wildlife conservation in the Black Hills. This great western pioneer would eventually found the town of Belle Fourche and win the confidence of none other than Teddy Roosevelt, the rough-riding 26th president of the United States. When Seth Bullock died in September 1919, his emaciated old frame aged far beyond his 70 years, he had become something of a legend in the land west of the Missouri River.

But as all of us know, legends don't die easy. While Seth Bullock's remains were buried atop Mount Moriah on a plot that overlooks Deadwood, many residents of the South Dakota community have reason to believe Seth's spirit still lives in the town he tamed. His place of residence? The Bullock Hotel.

Dating back to the 19th century, the Bullock Hotel is a living piece of Deadwood's history. Originally Seth Bullock's hardware store, the building was rebuilt as a hotel in 1895 after it was destroyed by fire. Seth oversaw the reconstruction of the hotel himself, wanting it to be distinct from the shoddy saloons and brothels that abounded in town. When it was finished, the Bullock Hotel stood as a fine example of Victorian luxury in a place where luxury was scarce. It was considered to be the best accommodation for miles around, at one time housing the likes of President Theodore Roosevelt. The pride of Deadwood while its founder was alive, the hotel began falling apart after Seth passed on.

Years brought careless owners, cobwebs in the corners, rot in the rafters and peeling paint. As time passed, the number of guests frequenting the hotel dropped off dramatically, and the building fell into anonymity, its rich past lost in the record of Deadwood's days. That was until 1988, when an energetic woman by the name of Mary Schmit bought the Bullock Hotel, planning to restore the establishment to its previous condition. The ensuing renovations brought out the ghost, or ghosts, of the Bullock Hotel.

First indications of the oddness in the hotel were minor. Renovators cursed about their frequently mislaid tools, wondering how the hammer they had just put down was now on the other side of the room, or why doors they had left open would slam shut behind them when there wasn't the slightest hint of a draft in the building. Before long, the occurrences in the hotel began getting weirder. Some workers claimed to hear the sound of cowboy boots on the wooden floor, spurs jangling in time with an invisible someone's slow, measured steps. Others claimed to hear a faint whisper through the clamor of renovations, a young girl saying their names in a barely audible voice. Among these workers' reports of strange happenings in the hotel were also the stories of sightings of Seth Bullock: a tall, skinny man in worn clothing, dusty boots and a beaten-up cowboy hat would just appear out of nowhere, only to vanish again in another instant.

While these experiences put off some renovators, they all knew that once the job was finished, they would be able to leave the hotel behind them. For those residents of Deadwood working in the Bullock Hotel after it was reopened, the spirits haunting the building would become a part of their day-to-day lives. Diane, who has worked at the Bullock Hotel's front desk for the last four years, has long-since grown accustomed to the building's peculiarity. "There've been numerous reports of strange happenings since I've started working here," an unfazed Diane says today. "I mean, anywhere from four to six stories a month."

Most of these stories involve the spirit of a friendly, helpful—if often mischievous—Seth Bullock. "One of the more famous encounters with Seth's spirit occurred a few years back," Diane says. "A little boy staying here with his family left his room late one night to go looking for his parents, who were in for a little gambling in the hotel's gaming hall. Well, this little boy ended up getting lost in the hotel. He was wandering aimlessly down one of the halls, crying his eyes out, when a tall man stopped him." What happened next is something of a local legend in Deadwood.

"What's the matter, boy?" the man asked gently.

"I can't find my mom," the child answered, trying his hardest to hold back his tears.

"Come now," the stranger said, smiling kindly, "your ma and pa are having a little bit of fun at cards. Why don't you be a big boy and let 'em wind down a bit." The tall man took off his worn cowboy hat and ran a hand through his dark hair. "Besides, it's late, and I'm sure your folks'd be cross if they knew you were wanderin' around when you should be sleepin'."

The man's gentle reasoning got through to the boy, and he nodded his silent agreement, suddenly realizing how sleepy he was. "Now, why don't you tell me what room you're stayin' in, and I'll take you there."

A few minutes later, the friendly stranger was standing in front of the suite door with the kid. "Thatta boy," he smiled at his ward, who had stopped crying, and had just produced a massive yawn. "Now have a good night's sleep." With that, the tall man in the cowboy hat patted the boy on the shoulder and said good-bye, waiting until the boy closed the door behind him before he walked away.

The next morning, the boy told his parents about the incident. Neither his mother nor father were happy that their child had been wandering through the hotel by himself, but they were grateful that he had met the good man in the hallway. It wasn't until they were checking out of the hotel later on that morning that they discovered who the man in the hallway actually was. "That's him mom! That's him!" the boy exclaimed, tugging on his mother's sleeve. Both mother and father looked to where their child was pointing; there on the wall was a portrait of Seth Bullock, the hotel's founder.

The boy's father laughed, "So we have a dead cowboy to thank for finding you, eh?"

But his mother, taking one look at the earnestness in her child's eyes, took her son seriously. "Are you sure that's the man, baby?"

That was when the woman working the desk piped up, "He isn't the only one that's seen him. Old Seth Bullock's ghost has been hanging around this hotel for years."

Diane wasn't working at the Bullock Hotel when this event transpired, but to this day, it stands as one of the most dramatic manifestations of Seth Bullock's ghost. Not that the old westerner limits his activity to helping lost children. "Seth never does any real harm," Diane says, "but he can be a bit on the mischievous side." Much of his mischief in the Bullock Hotel involves supernatural flirtation with the female guests. Diane recalls one of the old proprietor's recent pranks.

"In September 2002, a woman who was staying in the hotel with her husband had an encounter with Seth. The couple knew the stories about Seth's ghost, and when they were checking in, told me that they were hoping to see him. Well, they would never actually lay eyes on Seth when they were here, but it did seem like he paid them a visit. She told me about her experience when they were checking out the next day.

"This woman was woken up in the middle of the night by a hand on her hip. *Oh man,* she thought to herself, *my husband is being amorous again.* She turned over to face him, but found that he was fast asleep on his side, with his back to her. There was no possible way that he was the one who had just touched her. 'Yup,' I told her the next morning, 'that's Seth.'"

Indeed, Seth Bullock must have been quite a ladies' man during his earthly years, for many women staying at the hotel have reported similar experiences. "Some women taking showers have said that the door to the bathroom has swung open by itself," Diane says. "Others say that they've had strong feelings of being watched while combing their hair in the mirror. Not one of them has ever told me that they've felt threatened. It's actually sort of the opposite; they've felt almost amused at the attention of what they're certain is a friendly presence. Everyone who's had contact with Seth comes away with the feeling that they've shared a laugh with a kindly old man. Many of our guests have heard a story or two about Seth, and come to the hotel hoping to have a run-in with him."

But there is reason to believe that Seth's spirit isn't the only one that haunts the Bullock Hotel. Norm Stevens, who currently works just down the street at Miss Kitty's, was employed at the Bullock Hotel from 1989 to 1993. During that time, he had a number of supernatural experiences, and while he's certain that he brushed shoulders with the ghost of Seth Bullock on more than one occasion, he is convinced that his most poignant supernatural experiences were with another sprit. "Around the turn of the century, a typhoid epidemic went through Deadwood," Norm says. "It's a horrible way to go. The Bullock Hotel was used as a hospital at that time, and a lot of people died of typhoid in that building." Most of Norm's experiences in the hotel were with the spirit of a little girl, who he was convinced died of typhoid during the epidemic.

"When nobody was there and I was downstairs in my office doing paperwork, I'd hear her calling me, asking me what I was up to. It was always the same: 'Norman, what are you doing?' " Norm never felt threatened by the sound of the little girl's voice, but the hair would rise on the back of his neck nevertheless. There would never be any trace of a girl in the room.

The hotel's security system corroborated Norm's hunch that something was amiss in the basement of the hotel. "We had motion detectors down there," Norm says, "and they would often go off when nobody was down there. It happened more than once, where the motion detectors would indicate that something was moving downstairs, but the cameras monitoring the area wouldn't pick up a thing. Whatever was moving down there, it was invisible."

While Norm Stevens is sure the ghost of a typhoid victim haunts the hotel along with Seth Bullock, he states that there may very well be other spirits in the Bullock Hotel as well. If this is truly the case, at least it can be said that the ghost of Seth Bullock isn't alone. Perhaps the dead still consider the Bullock Hotel to be the best place to stay, just as visitors to Deadwood believed it to be when old Seth was still alive.

Easy Come, Easy Go

Henry Lambert stared at the five cards in front of him, trying his best to stop a smile from creeping to the corners of his mouth. There were five hearts in his hands, arranged in order from six to ten—a straight flush. Lambert let his eyes wander to the five other men sitting around the table, going from one man to the next, until they stopped on the famous Thomas Wright, one of the most celebrated card players on the frontier. *Here I am, out in New Mexico,* Lambert thought to himself, *playing poker at a high stakes table with the one and only Tom Wright, and I've got a straight flush in my hands.*

As far as Lambert was concerned, things couldn't get any better. *God knows, it's been long enough coming,* he thought as he looked around at the drunken revelry in his packed Cimarron saloon, *but I've finally made it.* The blithe Frenchman downed a shot of whiskey and looked back at the table, which was groaning under the weight of cash, gold and personal valuables gathered in the center. He looked at his cards again and smiled. *All mine.*

A French emigrant who had taken the trip across the Atlantic in the 1850s, Lambert was a young man with his head full of romantic notions about the American West when he arrived in the United States. He had left France determined to test his mettle in the wide-open wildness of the American frontier. Fanciful notions of the savage nobility of American Indians, the unrefined gallantry of Texans and the limitless possibilities of the western horizon were dancing through his mind. More than anything else, young Henry yearned for the wild places, and he made a promise to himself that as soon as he saved enough money to make the passage, he would try his luck in the California gold fields.

Fate, however, had different plans for him. For Henry Lambert had one talent that elevated him above other men, and it wasn't toughness, skill at cards or proficiency with a six-shooter. Henry Lambert could cook. Or maybe calling what he did in the kitchen "cooking" isn't quite right. The young Frenchman had been alive for over two decades and he had yet to meet a man who could throw together a better meal than he. Lambert was an artist, a genius, and anyone who tried his foie gras, glazed duck or quail eggs in Hollandaise sauce would be hard pressed to disagree.

Of course, Lambert didn't think that such a skill would serve him well on the rough fringes of frontier America, and he planned to use his talent purely as a means to get him to California. Getting work as a chef in an upscale New York restaurant, Henry Lambert began cooking in the New World with exactly this purpose in mind. But it wouldn't be that simple. The moment wealthy New Yorkers got a taste of Lambert's prodigious talents, he was elevated to culinary stardom. Every night, people clamored to get into the establishment where Henry cooked. Quickly gaining a reputation as one of the most gifted chefs in the city, Lambert attracted the attention of the wealthiest and most powerful in New York society.

Three years flew by in money-soaked succession, and before he was able to really take stock of his meteoric success, the young French chef was offered a job as the personal cook for none other than the president of the United States. And so it was that Henry Lambert got a job managing the White House kitchen when Abraham Lincoln won the presidency in

Gunfights and drunken punch-ups were a dime a dozen in many of the Old West's business establishments.

1860. Lambert stuck to the president for the next five years, pulling together the best meals he could for Lincoln while the Civil War raged across the United States. Who knows how long he would have remained in Washington had not things turned out they way they did? Did his dreams of lighting out West seem like a distant fantasy entertained by a much younger version of himself during his years at the White House? If they did, they come back strong in 1865. The very day it was announced that President Lincoln was dead, Lambert quit his job and left, turning his back on the East forever.

Yet the hopes he had for striking it rich in the hills of northern California were thwarted. While Henry was a brilliant chef, as a gold prospector he was inexperienced, uninformed and plain unlucky. Lambert was destitute within a year of arriving at Sacramento, having been conned, robbed and hoodwinked by every confidence man, highwayman and six-gun ne'er-do-well he came across. It turned out that the West wasn't nearly so grand as he had dreamt. So without a dollar or gold nugget to his name, Lambert went back to doing what he did best.

The once-famous chef got work in a San Francisco eatery and promptly began making magic of the local fare. Apparently, his skills weren't lost on the rough palates of frontier men, and the establishment he worked at was soon bursting at the rafters with every gambler, gunfighter and gold digger that could fit in the building. One of the customers, a wealthy New Mexican financier, enjoyed his meal so much that he walked into the kitchen after he was finished and offered Lambert an exorbitant sum to be his personal cook. Lambert didn't have to think about it too long; taking a final look at the cramped and chaotic kitchen he had worked in, the chef walked out with his new employer, taking the next train out to Cimarron, New Mexico.

He made more money working for his new employer than he did working for the president, and after a few years Henry had saved up a substantial sum. It was then that the master chef decided to open up an establishment of his own. Opening up Lambert's Saloon and Billiard Club in the late 1870s, Henry suddenly found himself in the position to cook his goose's golden eggs and indulge his lifelong fascination with the Wild West. For Henry's saloon did a raucous business in the bustling town of Cimarron, which was located on the last stretch of the Santa Fe Trail.

Lambert's establishment bore hardly any resemblance to past eateries he had worked in. More a frontier drinking room than a restaurant, Lambert's selection in whiskies and ales dwarfed his sparse menu of French cuisine. Most of the men who stepped into his saloon were more interested in cards and booze than fine food, and it wasn't long before Lambert's Saloon became a famous gathering place for some of the worst men the southwest had to offer. After its first few years of business, Lambert's operation was so successful that he added 30 more hotel rooms to it and renamed it the St. James Hotel. The most infamous of the Old West's perfidious pantheon would eventually walk through the St. James' front door—men such as Clay Allison, Wyatt Earp, Billy the Kid and Pat Garret all spent time under Lambert's roof at one time or another.

In turn, Lambert traded in his spatula for a six-shooter and took to joining his dubious celebrity guests for booze and cards, fancying himself an honorary member of the six-gun brotherhood that whooped it up in his bar nightly. He was probably the most permissive barkeeper in all of Cimarron, and it is said that 26 men were killed in drunken shootouts that erupted within the saloon. Legend has it that the ceiling had to be replaced after the first couple of years because of the 400-some bullet holes punched through it.

Lambert was probably happiest during this period of his life. Laughing, drinking and gambling with the same scoundrels he worshipped, the former cook drank up the company of these frontiersmen with unbridled zeal. But like all good things, his days under the western sun did not last. The end of his glory days came quickly, in all the time it took for a man to throw down five cards on a table.

Though Thomas Wright carried a six-shooter, he never used it. One of the more accomplished gamblers west of the Mississippi, Wright made his living at the card tables across the frontier. He played in practically every gambling house from Tombstone to Dodge City and was known for his fair play and his outsized personality. So it was that Wright was one of those few men who could boast at having won the last dollar off murderous gamblers like Ben Thompson and Doc Holliday without a single altercation. He couldn't have imagined his clean track record was about to change when he was introduced to a drunk and merry Henry Lambert, who gave Wright an affectionate hug when he met him.

For that matter, Lambert couldn't have imagined it either. Indeed, with the six-to-ten straight flush in his hand, the former cook couldn't imagine anything besides the small fortune he was about to win—about to win, no less, from Thomas Wright. The pot built steadily as the bets went around the table. Men threw in hundred dollar bills, watches, gold nuggets, precious jewels—by the time it came around to Lambert for the second time, the chef decided to make a grand statement about the cards in his hand. Basking in the attention of the spectators, the soused man let a moment of dramatic silence pass before he made his bet. "I would like to bet the title deed of this hotel."

Much to Lambert's delight, a collective gasp went through the gambling room, as if the St. James itself had drawn its breath in disbelief. By the time the chef wrote up a hasty deed on a piece of paper, all of the other men at the table had folded, unable or unwilling to match the excessive bet. All, that is, except Tom Wright.

Eyeing up Henry Lambert with a lopsided grin stretched across his face, Wright reached into his jacket pocket and pulled out a wad of folded hundred dollar bills that looked thick enough to stop a bullet. The legendary gambler paused for a moment before he threw the money down. "I wouldn't normally ask, but you sure you want to do this, Frenchy?"

Lambert felt beads of sweat forming on his brow in spite of himself. "You're bluffing," was all he could get out.

"So be it." Tom Wright said as he threw the cash onto the middle of the table. "I call."

Lambert laid his straight flush down, finally allowing his smile to break out into a joyful guffaw. "Beat that, ye' old card shark!" he hollered at his opponent. Henry was just about to lean forward and grab his loot when Tom Wright threw his cards down: he was holding a royal flush. All spades.

"Nothing personal, Frenchy," Tom said to the suddenly pale chef, "but I'll be wanting you out of here by tomorrow. A bet's a bet, after all."

Tom reached forward to grab the loot when Lambert snapped. "You cheat!" the enraged Frenchman roared at his opponent. "There's no way you could've drew a royal flush." Lambert was stammering as he spoke, unable to come to terms with his loss. When Tom made another movement to take his winnings, Lambert ordered two of the house toughs to hold him back. "Search his sleeves!" he yelled at his thugs. "I'll bet anything he's got cards in his jacket."

"I wouldn't be making any more bets for a while if I were you," Tom said to Lambert as the two burly men rifled through his jacket. There were no cards on him. "Well, that settles it then," he said. "Fair and square, eh Pierre? I'm goin' upstairs to get some sleep."

"Get out of my hotel!" Lambert screamed at the professional gambler as he walked away.

"Hell Henry, you can't kick me out of my own place," Tom answered over his shoulder.

A few men in the saloon laughed; Lambert flipped his lid. An instant later, the chef reached down to his hip with shaking hands, yanked his shooting iron and fired, blowing a hole through Tom's back. Silence descended over the hotel as the patrons took in the spectacle of Wright in his death throes on the saloon floor. But no one was more shaken than the perpetrator of the capital crime. Unable to soak in what he had done, Lambert dropped his gun and dashed out of the saloon, leaving a writhing Tom Wright behind him. "Well," someone said, "we best take him to his room."

A few men stepped forward, lifting the dying man off the floor and taking him to his hotel suite: room 18. If Wright was a congenial man throughout his life, there was nothing graceful about the way he left the world. Thrashing violently in blood-soaked sheets, the gambler unleashed his pain and anger in a series of profane epithets, calling down the town of Cimarron, the establishment he was gunned down in, and, most of all, the "yellow-bellied Frenchman" who shot him in the back. A doctor was called in to see if anything could be done, but Wright was quickly deemed beyond help. A priest followed, intent on giving the dying man his last rites, but Tom pulled his revolver and shouted every curse he could think of at the rapidly retreating priest. "Hellfire if my soul ain't damned beyond any prayer!" the livid man shrieked at the holy man's back. "But by Lucifer and his burning host, I swear I'll come back to torment that lousy Frenchman! I swear it!" At that moment, there wasn't a man in the bar who didn't believe him. Tom was dead before the night was up.

Lambert returned to his hotel after a brief hiatus, planning to manage the establishment again. But things at the St. James would never be the same. For one, Henry Lambert had lost his jovial air. No longer did patrons hear his delirious laughter ring through the hotel on crowded nights; no longer did he walk amongst his frontier clientele with his put-on swagger, pressing palms and buying drinks. Indeed, Lambert spent more and more time in the confines of his kitchen, sitting in silence for entire evenings with a bottle of whiskey in his hands. In the end, this eager western enthusiast found his own frontier experience too much to digest, and the rest of his days were spent in a haunted and heavy silence.

But Lambert wasn't the only one who was haunted by the deceased gambler. Soon after Tom Wright passed on, employees and patrons of the St. James Hotel became convinced that the dead man's spirit remained in the hotel to see through his dying curse. His presence was said to be especially strong in the first few years after he died. Employees would tell stories about being struck by some invisible force while they were working; bottles of booze frequently flew off shelves and across the room, shattering against the barroom walls. It wasn't uncommon for men playing cards at the table where Wright was dealt his last hand to bolt out of their seats and run out of the hotel screaming, later saying that they felt a pair of ice cold hands close around their throats.

Yet of all the strange things that occurred, the most terrifying phenomena occurred in room 18. Patrons unfortunate enough to sleep in room 18 would never make it through the night. Invariably, they would come running out sometime in the early hours with some story about "the angry man at the foot of the bed" or the thick cloud of menacing mist that floated through the room, turning the bedchamber into a veritable ice box. It wasn't long before Lambert had the room locked up for good, but even then, those suites adjacent to the cursed room had their fair share of strange goings-on, and Lambert would warn guests staying in them about the unfriendly ghost that was known to appear there.

Things went from bad to worse at the St. James Hotel. As the phenomena in the hotel intensified, Tom Wright's last words took on the weight of legend. "It's the spirit of Tom Wright up there in room 18," locals would say. "He said he'd come back from the dead to stick it to ol' Lambert; I guess that's what he's done." Others offered theories on the dead gambler's determination to see that Lambert made good on his bet, saying that if Wright couldn't take what was owed him in life, his spirit would do his darndest after death. And maybe Wright would have driven Lambert out of the hotel after all, if Lambert's wife, Mary, hadn't passed away when she did.

By all accounts, the paranormal activity at the St. James lessened considerably after Mary Lambert died. While strange and unpleasant things still occurred regularly in room 18, bottles had stopped flying across the barroom and the attacks on patrons dropped off dramatically. Wright's angry ghost stopped appearing in the rooms next to 18. Moreover, other, more pleasant, stories began circulating about the St. James. Employees grew conscious of a mysterious helper that would help them with the work around the hotel. Chambermaids walking into rooms they were about to clean would find beds made with crisp, clean sheets, while the dirty linens would be piled neatly beside the door. Dishes suddenly acquired a mysterious tendency to clean themselves, and Henry Lambert put away the bottle and took up cooking again, once more putting his talents to good use with the wide array of new dishes he put on the menu.

Guests noticed the change as well. Some said they spotted a kind-looking middle-aged woman framed by a warm and comforting light. Anyone who spotted her would talk about the undeniable sense of well-being they felt when they saw her. Business picked up in the St. James Hotel once again, and while room 18 was still off limits, the air around the locked door still whispering an intangible and ominous promise, there was almost no trace of the vicious spirit that haunted the hotel throughout much of the 1880s.

The popular theory is that the spirit of Mary Lambert, always kind and gentle while alive, had taken up residence in her husband's hotel after she died, hoping to help the poor man deal with the sins of his past. Somehow, she was able to ease Wright's angry presence with her own good-hearted influence. In this sense, the St. James became something of a paranormal battleground, where one woman's gentle ghost somehow managed to keep another, fiercely malevolent, spirit in check.

Ever since, and to this day, owners, employees and guests of the St. James have expressed awareness of this two-sided ghostly element in the hotel. On one hand, there is the darkness that resides in the still-barred room 18, while on the other, there is the calming spirit of Mary Lambert who seems to have free reign over the rest of the building. Management has done everything it can to placate the angry Wright, while keeping Mary happy as well. Room 18 has been stocked with three of Tom Wright's favorite things in the world: a pack of playing cards, a shot glass and a bottle of Jack Daniels. Meanwhile, guests staying in Mary Lambert's room are told only to make sure that they shut the window before they go to sleep. An open window is said to be the only thing that irritates Mary, who has been known to tap on the window until sleeping guests wake up and close it.

A small price to pay for protection from Tom Wright's vengeance.

5

Go West, Young Man

Hollenberg Station and the Ghosts of the Pony Express

The word went out across the Missouri frontier in March 1860:

> WANTED—Young, skinny, wiry fellows, not over 18. Must be expert riders, to risk death daily. Orphans preferred.

Newspapers in every county throughout the state printed the ad, put out by the major freighting company Russell, Majors and Waddell. It was the first call for riders for the Pony Express, the legendary western mail service that would cut through 2000 miles of prairie and mountain to link California to the rest of the Union. The service was born from necessity. In 1860, the telegraph went only as far west as St. Joseph, Missouri. Mail to California went overland by stagecoach or via steamship down and around the continent from New York to San Francisco; both routes took over 20 days to complete.

A more efficient method was needed. As the population of California reached half a million souls and political turmoil in the East set the battle lines between North and South, the need for quicker communication became more important. So it was that Russell, Majors and Waddell developed the Pony Express. The idea was to set up a relay route where a succession of accomplished horsemen would be waiting at stations along the way. Riders carried a bag full of mail along the Pony Express route, passing it on to the

An engraving of a Pony Express rider passing the men erecting the first transcontinental telegraph. The telegraph rendered the service obsolete.

next rider at every station. Thus the mail was to be relayed from St. Louis to Sacramento at the speed of a near-constant gallop.

The Pony Express officially opened on April 3, 1860, and the first westbound shipment made the journey from St. Joseph to Sacramento in nine days and 23 hours, under half the time it took for stagecoach mail to cover the distance. Though the Pony Express lasted only 19 months, put out of

Hollenberg Station, built in the late 1850s, was once a stop for the Pony Express. After the station shut down, a phantom rider began appearing.

business when a telegraph line was lain across the country, it left a lasting impression on the popular imagination.

American writers and reporters made the Pony Express riders into a unique kind of rough-riding hero: a determined equestrian who was reckless, dauntless and as fast as the prairie wind—a Hermes on horseback, delivering the word of civilization across wild America. Although 19th-century writers may have been taking some creative liberties with the facts, the facts alone were still remarkable. Pony Express riders were typically teenagers and young men, small in stature so that the galloping broncos they rode were not taxed by extra weight, endowed with outsized courage to deal with the dangers of their job. The riders were expected to make it through their stretches as fast as possible. Depending upon where they were stationed, riders covered anywhere from 70 to 100 miles before passing the bag on, going the whole way at a full gallop. They switched horses at relay stations dotted along the express route every 10 to 20 miles, stopping only long enough to get a fresh mount and take a quick swig of water before pressing on. The stops at these stations were never longer than two minutes. Yet even at this pace, riders were often hard pressed to outrun danger.

Many of the riders had to make their way through hostile Indian territory and lawless lands. They were hounded by fears of Indian attack and banditry—fears that became reality for more than one rider galloping along the mail route. There is the story of young Billy Tate, only 14 years old, who ran into a Paiute war party while riding through Ruby Valley in Nevada. No one can say how the fight played out, but it must have been a hell of one. When they found Billy's body, he was lying dead behind the bullet-ridden carcass of his horse—seven dead Paiute warriors were strewn around him. Honoring the bravery of Billy's last stand, the Paiute left his scalp intact and his mailbag untouched.

The Paiute of the Nevada Territory took another victim a few months later when they ambushed a 19-year-old named Bart Riles as he made his way from Cold Springs to Edwards Creek. Catching Bart unawares, the Paiutes opened up at practically point blank range, blowing two holes through the Pony Express rider's chest. Somehow, the mortally wounded boy still managed to get away, turning his horse around and galloping back to the Cold Springs station. He held onto life just long enough to make it to Cold Springs. That shipment of mail arrived in Sacramento slightly later than scheduled, stained with the blood of the boy who died to get it there.

It was touchy work, and those who did not die performing it certainly earned their spurs as some of the toughest men of the West. Before he was "Buffalo Bill," a 15-year-old William Cody rode the 76-mile stretch between Red Butte and Three Crossings, Wyoming. Later on in his life, when he was putting on his Wild West Show all over the world, Buffalo Bill would refer to his Pony Express days as some of the most dangerous in his long and eventful life.

Shut down only a year and a half after it opened, the Pony Express was quickly enshrined within the canon of American legend. Even as its stations were abandoned and dismantled, the Pony Express took on heroic proportions in America. Eastern readers, thrilled at the idea of the frontier, read dozens of dime novel adventures featuring the bold riders of the Express. Yet the legacy of the Pony Express wasn't limited to the written page. For on the plains of northeastern Kansas, in a building near the town of Hanover, Washington County, something strange and unnatural came to being—a bizarre phenomenon that would continue long after the Pony Express itself expired.

The Hollenberg Station was built in the late 1850s by Gerat Hollenberg, a German immigrant who hoped to free himself from farming by setting up a general store. He saw some success over the next few years, supplying the local farmers with dry goods and farming supplies, but it wasn't until 1860, when Russell, Majors and Waddell announced that the Pony Express route would cut through the small Kansas town, that Gerat smelled a real chance to make a

By 1941 Hollenberg Station was the only Pony Express stop still located on its original site—apparently a haunted site.

buck. Offering the Pony Express his store as a relay station, Gerat added to the building, constructing sleeping quarters for riders on the second floor and a large stable for the Express horses. The mail service took the man up on his offer, and Gerat made a killing over the next 19 months, catering to the rush of Express riders that raced east and west through his property.

Traffic through the area greatly diminished when the Pony Express went out of business, and Gerat was forced to

scale down his operation. It soon became obvious, however, that things at Hollenberg Station would never go
back to what they were. Strange noises were heard in the
middle of the night; more than once Gerat was woken by
the sound of galloping hooves tearing right by his home.
Though common when the Pony Express was in operation,
the noises made no sense after it had been shut down. Gerat
couldn't think of a single farmer who would even consider
streaking through his property in the middle of the night
just for kicks.

On other nights, he woke to the sound of a distant shout,
of a young man yelling "Mail coming in!"—the same signal
that was shouted out when Pony Express riders approached
the former station, warning the next rider to be ready to go.
But now, no exhausted youngster appeared out of the darkness. There was no frantic exchange of mailbags. There were
no cries of encouragement as the fresh rider tore away—
there was only silence, the prairie wind and a frightened
Gerat Hollenberg, standing alone in his nightclothes, peering
into the darkness for some sign of the phantom rider.

These occurrences grew more dramatic as time passed.
Every year, the hooves got louder when they went by. The
shouts of the mysterious rider got clearer, more pronounced.
Gerat Hollenberg was a God-fearing man, and he made it a
habit not to think too deeply about things he didn't understand, so very little was said about these phenomena while
Hollenberg was alive. By the time Hollenberg passed away, he
had established himself as one of Washington County's premier citizens, making a sizeable fortune in real estate, serving
three terms in the Kansas legislature and founding the
nearby town of Hanover. Yet very few people knew of the

bizarre happenings that continued to occur at the old Hollenberg Station.

For a long time, the stories of the goings-on at the station were kept alive by those young residents of Hanover who ventured out to the station after dark to witness the phantom rider for themselves. It wasn't until many years later, in 1941, when the Kansas legislature turned the station into a state historic site, that the phenomena at the Hollenberg Station became more widely known. By that time, Hollenberg Station had become recognized as the only Pony Express stop that was still standing on its original site, and visitors came from all over the country to see it. The Hollenberg Station is an impressive historical resource, providing visitors with dynamic perspectives on the Pony Express and its time. But the most-talked-about relics at Hollenberg aren't contained within its wooden walls.

He appears to those people who tarry at the station grounds long enough for sunset. The first sign of his approach is the sound of galloping hooves in the distance, followed by a shout—"Mail coming in!" The voice sounds as if it comes from a great distance. And then, in the next moment, he appears: a rider hunched over the back of a sorrel horse, moving impossibly fast. He appears to be more of a blur than anything else, mostly transparent, the details of the rider and the animal obscured by the dim light and the speed of his approach. Before witnesses can even let out an astonished gasp, he's gone, flashing by the station and into the darkness west.

The phantom rider appears for only a handful of seconds but has left such an impression on those who have seen him that Hollenberg Station has become one of Kansas' most famous haunted locales, written up by more than one super-natural enthusiast and investigated by numerous paranormal groups. No one has been able to determine who exactly this rider is or why he continues to gallop past the Hollenberg Station so long after the Pony Express has been disbanded. Indeed, these individuals have raised more questions than they've been able to answer.

Is the ghost a spirit of one of the riders who was killed on the Express line? Or could he be a rider that was so thrilled by his work that he left some abstract and intangible part of himself on the mail route, a manifestation that continues to ride the Pony Express route today? Furthermore, why was Gerat Hollenberg only able to hear the apparition, never once claiming to have laid eyes upon it? By all accounts, the Pony Express phantom has gotten more active as the years have passed. Could it be that the entire Pony Express route is haunted by the spirits of the youngsters who carried out their historic work, but as each of the stations has been demol-ished or moved, the ghosts' collective energy has gathered in ever-greater concentration around Hollenberg? Like most questions regarding the supernatural, any answer is pure conjecture. We can only say for sure that something beyond our understanding continues to occur around Hollenberg Station, something that is unquestionably and inexplicably linked to the legendary Pony Express.

Vallecito Station

It was a clear night in the Anza Borrego Desert. A thin sliver of a moon hung in the starry sky, glittering in marked contrast to the rock, dirt and sagebrush of the California desert. But for a few rattlesnakes slithering through the bush and a solitary coyote howling at the heavens, the night was silent. The four horsemen saddled up behind a high outcropping of boulders did little to disturb this quiet. Masked and armed to the teeth with shotguns, rifles and revolvers, the riders sat as still as statues, looking intently through the darkness at the single road stretching across the desert below them.

One of the masked riders finally broke the silence. "Damnit Luke, when did you say that coach was coming by?" the man growled at the leader of the outfit. "My rear is gettin' sore with all this sitting." The captain of the band scanned the dark horizon with an attentive eye, giving no indication that he heard his cranky confederate's complaint. "I said Luke," the grizzled bandit spoke up again, "does this bleedin' coach even come through here? I can't see a damn thing for miles."

This time, the leader of the foursome hissed for silence. Squinting hard into the darkness, the man stood in his stirrups and leaned forward, trying to get a better look at whatever had caught his attention. His horse snorted as he sat back down in the saddle, cocked the lever of his Winchester rifle and shot a toothy grin at the man who had been pestering him. "Time to quit your yappin', Bill," he said, "a wagon's comin' fast from the west. It's time for the show." The four men waited until the wagon was just below them before they put their spurs to their horses and descended on the coach. The infamous holdup in the Anza Borrego had begun.

The Butterfield Station (above), in Oak Grove, San Diego County, was another station on the Pony Express line.

It was the summer of 1857, and the bandits were riding down on a stagecoach said to be hauling $65,000 east to St. Louis. Luke told his band that the plan was to take the loot and ride hard for Vallecito Station several miles to the east. Once there, they were to divide the take four ways and split up for good, each lighting off with over $15,000 in his saddlebags. That was the plan anyway, but the heist in the Anza Borrego turned out to be a much more complicated affair—

an ugly debacle of betrayal and bloodshed that left a stain on the desert that many believe remains today, manifested in the ghostly apparitions that appear in Vallecito Station.

"Don't even think about using that thing, boy!" Luke roared at the stagecoach guard, whose hand was slowly closing around the handle of his shotgun. "We've got four guns with your name stamped on 'em. Just make the move and we'll open them up!"

The man riding shotgun hesitated, his mind racing over odds of survival, the value of his life and his current standing with the Almighty. Casting one more glance at the four loaded guns trained on him, he decided that he wasn't willing to die over someone else's money. He put the shotgun down on the wagon floorboards and raised his arms into the sky.

"Smart move boy, keep listening to that voice in your head and you might live to see the morning." Luke nodded at two of the bandits, who rode up to the coach, shot the lock off the door and began emptying it, one bag at a time. They didn't stop until $65,000 in gold coins hung from their horses' saddles. Luke tipped his hat at the driver and the guard before he gave the word to his band, and the four riders galloped away, their forms fading quickly in the darkness.

But as soon as the riders turned their backs on the coach, the guard was moved by a sudden change of heart. He picked his shotgun up off the coach floor, stood up and aimed it carefully at one of the riders. The rider had just vanished from sight when the guard pulled the trigger, but his aim was true—enough of the shotgun blast had found its mark. The bandit slumped lifeless in his saddle. He had been riding one of the horses that was loaded up with gold, and Luke wheeled his horse around to take the animal by the reins, leading it to where the two surviving brigands waited. "That treacherous bastard," the man on the other gold-laden packhorse hissed in the darkness. "I say we ride back and shoot them both dead."

"Why now, what would we gain from killing those men?" Luke said to his enraged accomplice. "I mean, if I were you, I'd be worried about adding any more dead men to my earthly sins."

"What the hell are you talkin' about Luke?"

"I'm talkin' about the hell you're going to, fool."

With these words, Luke nodded at the third man, Bill, who was holding a revolver to the back of the bandit's head. A second later, another gun blast tore through the night, and the unsuspecting man tumbled from his saddle and into oblivion, shot dead by his traitorous companion. "Good shootin', Bill," Luke said, "I knew you had it in you."

The two men got off their horses and mounted the animals carrying the gold. Galloping the entire way to the Vallecito Station stage stop, built in an Anza Borrego oasis, Luke and Bill stopped once somewhere along the way to bury their haul. To this day, no one knows exactly where the treasure was buried, although many have looked. According to legend, the treasure still lies somewhere in the Anza Borrego, left behind by the two treacherous bandits who didn't live long enough to reclaim it.

After the pair hid the gold, they rode up into the Vallecito Station, where they sat down in a shady corner of the adobe structure to celebrate their perfidious heist. Ordering shot after shot of rotgut whiskey, they drank to their newfound wealth and the demise of their confederates. "Forget about 'em!" Bill was heard saying at one point, "they were about as useful as an Indian in harvest."

"Well," Luke responded, "thanks to those two, I'll never have to draw my gun again. It ain't nothing but the good life for me now, Bill."

Luke could have no idea how mistaken he was. For while the two were able to pull off their scheme flawlessly, their plans failed to take into account the dearth of the most valuable commodity in any partnership: trust. It wasn't long before their whiskey-fueled exuberance turned into besotted paranoia. Luke's casual glances at those in the room got Bill to wondering if Luke had devised a plot to get rid of him as well. He kept convincing himself that a man with a loaded gun was standing right behind him, ready to shoot, and he was unable to go five seconds at a time without throwing worried glances over his shoulder. Of course, as Luke began to worry about what had gotten into Bill, he noticed that his partner's laughter was growing forced, uneasy. The usually composed bandit leader became wary.

Finally, Luke spoke up. "What's gotten into you, man?" the drunken bandit slurred. "You worried a priest is gonna show up or what?"

Bill looked closely at the man sitting opposite him, his eyes squinting. "Why is that? I'm just taking a look around, you got somethin' 'gainst that?" The robber glared across the table through whiskey eyelids. "Or are you hoping to catch me unawares?"

It was then that Luke saw the streak of hatred smeared across Bill's face, and instantly became aware that his partner was packing a loaded Peacemaker at his hip. *The bastard intends to shoot me,* Luke thought as his hand fell under the table to where his own shooting iron was strapped. He asked his next question in slow, measured tones, his palm clasped tightly around the handle of his Colt 45. "You ain't thinking of doing anything stupid, are ya Bill?"

Not another word was said; Bill rose to his feet and hauled his revolver from its holster. But he was too slow. Luke, still sitting, skinned his gun first, firing two bullets into Bill's stomach before the man could get a single shot off. Luke got up and started to walk out of Vallecito Station even as his former friend fell to the ground, clutching at his perforated belly with a blood-soaked hand. The fight, however, was not quite over. Just as Bill began losing focus, he picked his pistol up off the floor and fired at the man who had just shot him. His bullet found its mark, and Luke fell dead at the threshold of the building; a moment later, Bill collapsed as well, breathing his last as his blood spread across the Vallecito Station floor.

The stagecoach that the bandits had robbed arrived at Vallecito Station later that night, and it wasn't long before bystanders put the details of the gunfight together. That same night, almost everyone at the station went out looking for the buried gold, hoping to strike it rich on the bandits' ill-gotten gains. Yet no one found it. The story of the lost gold in the Anza Borrego spread throughout the West over the following years, and people came from all over looking for the buried treasure. Seasons became years, which turned to decades, and still, the gold of the Anza Borrego went unclaimed. Time turned the robbery and brutal murders that followed into one of the legends of the Old West, and future generations saw the hidden gold in the desert as more of a folktale than a tangible treasure waiting to be discovered. The promise of gold wasn't the only thing that made the Anza Borrego heist into legend.

People began to talk about strange goings-on in Vallecito Station soon after Luke and Bill killed each other. The first of these reports came from passengers on the Butterfield Overland Stage. Established in 1858, the Butterfield Stage offered a route to travelers making the long trip between St. Louis and San Francisco, and it passed very near the Vallecito Station. While the Butterfield Overland Stage was in business, from 1858 to 1861, Vallecito Station saw its busiest time, and it was during this period that the legend of the phantom gunfighters was born.

To those visitors stopping at the station during daylight hours, the spirits manifested themselves with disembodied footsteps—the sound of spurs jingling as an invisible presence makes its way to the adobe structure only to fall silent just before the doorway. Others sitting in the sweltering heat claimed to be seized by a sudden cold spell so severe that it made the hairs stand up on the back of necks and breath turn to visible vapor. The cold lasted only for minutes, and occurred only in the same corner where Luke and Bill sat after they held up the stagecoach in 1857.

Visitors to the station during evening hours were in for even more startling experiences. The spirits of Vallecito seemed to acquire greater strength after the sun went down. It was then that Luke and Bill acquired form, appearing as faint apparitions to travelers. Shocked eyewitnesses could only stare at the slightly transparent image of Luke as he took his last steps towards the Vallecito Station exit. Others looked horrified at the faintly luminescent form of Bill lying face down on the same ground where he fell. The Civil War brought an end to the Butterfield Line, and the Vallecito Station was deserted, left to bake, forgotten, in the southern California sun.

San Diego County purchased the station and surrounding oasis in 1934, almost a century later, and rebuilt the crumbling building from its ruins. Vallecito was turned into a campground for motorists in the Anza Borrego—once more a rest stop for travelers. Apparently, the years did nothing to resolve Luke and Bill's differences. For as soon as visitors returned to Vallecito, so too were sightings of their ghosts reported.

They were seen most often by those camped close to Vallecito Station. Witnesses claimed to hear the footsteps from their tents: the sound of a man in boots and spurs walking in the adobe building. Many of those who went out to investigate claimed that they saw a man with a wide-brimmed hat on his head walking out of the station before vanishing in thin air. And sure enough, witnesses brave enough to investigate after having laid eyes on this disappearing bandit have seen the shimmering image of luckless Bill lying face down in the same corner he was shot.

While most sightings of these long-dead outlaws occur within the station, a few campers claimed to have heard the jangling spurs outside. The campgrounds closest to the station have been rich ground for paranormal phenomena. Over the years, many campers at these sites have heard the sound of the phantom outlaw's footsteps walking through their campsites. For some, the experiences have been terrifying affairs, where the footsteps have grown louder and louder, stopping just outside their tents. Many have lain in terrified silence throughout the night, too frightened to move, convinced that someone was standing just outside. Those able to gather enough courage to confront the presence outside have emerged from their tents to the sight of the empty night.

Has the ghost of the dead bandit finally managed to leave the building where he was shot dead? Does his spirit remain behind in the hope of finding his buried treasure? Or could this lonely ghost be looking for some sort of company in the desert night? Who knows, perhaps he finds it. For there is one other famous ghost in the oasis: the White Lady of Vallecito.

The White Lady

She is seen during the twilight hours: a glimmering apparition of a woman in a resplendent white gown, rising from her unmarked grave behind the adobe building and floating to the front entrance, where she remains for several moments before vanishing into the air. She is the White Lady of Vallecito, a famous phantom that has haunted the old station since she met her end there, over 150 years ago.

Her name was Eileen O'Connor, a young woman from the East who was making her way to Sacramento to marry her beau, a gold prospector who had just struck it rich in the California gold fields. Booking passage on the Butterfield Line, Eileen fell ill sometime during the hard journey, and by the time her coach arrived at the Vallecito Station she was too weak to continue. Her fellow passengers carried her to a bed in the back of the station, where she was tended to by the station employees. They did all they could, but it was soon evident that she was beyond any help. The third day after she arrived, O'Connor succumbed to her fever.

The people who had been taking care of her went through her possessions to see if they could get any information about her identity. Yet all she had was a satin wedding dress and a locket containing a photograph of her beau. So it was that they dressed O'Connor in her wedding gown and buried her in an anonymous grave behind the station. When her loved ones discovered what had happened, they didn't have the heart to have her remains exhumed, and she remained in her lonely plot behind station, far away from friends and family.

Eileen O'Connor did not rest peacefully. The sightings of the White Lady of Vallecito began to be reported soon after she was interred. No one knows the exact date she rose from the grave for the first time, but it was said to be during a spectacular sunset sometime in 1859. She rose under a bloodred sky, her pale face completely expressionless except for a deep sadness that emanated from her eyes. Glowing faintly in the darkening desert, her transparent apparition drifted over the dirt to the front of the station. Several horrified witnesses stared in utter silence as the White Lady stood there, waiting, it seemed, for something to arrive. She remained hovering for a few minutes before she began to fade. And then she was gone, leaving nothing but a dry wind behind her.

It was the first of countless appearances. The White Lady was seen by numerous passengers of the Butterfield Line until 1861, when the company abandoned Vallecito Station. We can only guess if she continued to appear in front of the station during its long period of abandonment, but as soon as people began visiting the station again when it was made into a park in 1938, stories of the White Lady began to circulate again. Is her spirit, unable to cope with the tragedy of her death, waiting for a carriage to take her to her fiancé? If so, it is fitting that she keeps company with the bandit ghost of

Vallecito, who, like the spirit of O'Connor, met his end just before he would claim his treasure.

Ghosts of the Yuma Territorial Prison

Death is the tyrant that strikes fear into the hearts of most of the convicts. It means those that are not claimed and are without friends will lie beneath the barren plot just outside the penitentiary—the convict's cemetery. Piles of rock shaped like a grave with a plain slab giving the name and number mark the final resting place. Services are brief at a convict's funeral. There are no mourners, no tears, no flowers—a simple burial service by a minister or priest, and that is all.

The Tucson Citizen,
November 24, 1906

The Yuma Territorial Prison had been open for over 30 years when this bleak account of death within the isolated penitentiary was penned by a Tucson journalist. By then, it was clear that the old rock and adobe prison was nearing the end of its service. Crumbling and overcrowded, the old prison was a physical reminder of a bygone age—a relic from a time when there were more tumbleweeds than people in the southwestern corner of the country, and justice was just as likely to be administered with the wrong end of a six-shooter as it was through due process of law.

The prison's first cells were built by seven unfortunate convicts from the Yuma County jail in the early summer of 1876. They were brought to the site throughout that May and June, marched through the desert shackled and chained, supervised under gunpoint as they broke rock and piled rock to form their own prison cells in the middle of the Yuma desert. We can only imagine what these men must have been thinking as they groaned and sweated under the sweltering heat, constructing the walls that would soon enclose them.

These cells were finished on July 1 that year, just in time for monsoon season. While the seven convicts were imprisoned, they put up with the extremities of the Yuma Desert's harsh climate, where temperatures could get as high as 120° F in midday, turning their small cluster of adobe cells into sun-baked ovens. When the rains came, water thundered down on the cells, pouring in through every crack in the poorly constructed building. A stay in the Yuma Prison was hardly luxurious, and over the years, the prison grew with the number of convicts in the territory: cells were constructed to accommodate the increasing number of badmen riding into the Yuma Territory.

Every sort of person did time in the cramped cells. There were mankillers, robbers, swindlers and perverts; drunkards and gamblers; victims and innocents. While the prison was active, 3069 prisoners, 29 of them women, served sentences in the territorial prison. Not everyone made it out of the prison alive. One hundred and eleven convicts died in their cells, looking out at the world through barred windows

during the last moments of their lives. It is believed that a
few of the spirits of these unlucky few still haunt the Yuma
Territorial Prison, which operates today as one of Arizona's
state historic parks.

Many believe the ghost of John Ryan to be the most active
spirit that haunts the former prison. No one can say who saw
him first. It may have been a tourist wandering through the
park in the not-too-distant past, or it may have been a convict unlucky enough to be thrown into cell 14 when the penitentiary was still being used. Whatever the case, Ryan's ghost
manifested itself the way it always has: a faint white figure
pacing within the darkness of the cell, two dimly shining
eyes, the sound of nervous footsteps walking back and forth,
a sudden drop in temperature.

John Ryan was the first man to die in the Yuma Territorial
Prison. As depraved a man as the West had ever produced,
Ryan wandered in from Iowa during the 1890s, trying to make
his way as a miner on the frontier. He was successful enough
at this endeavor to start a family, getting married shortly
after arriving and fathering three children with his young
wife. But, as they say, you can take the man out of the place,
but you can't take the devil out of the man, and whatever
inner demons John Ryan thought he left behind in Iowa
came back with a vengeance on the wild periphery of the
United States.

Ryan fell into debauchery soon after his third child was
born, spending more and more time at the nearest saloon,
filling his gut with acrid frontier whiskey and gambling away
what little money he had. We can only guess at what kind of
madness possessed him, but by the end of 1899, he hit rock
bottom. The record shows only that he was arrested for

committing a "crime against nature" and was sentenced to five years in the Yuma Territorial Prison on September 28, 1900.

Where some murderers, robbers and con artists might have received a certain degree of respect in western jail houses, men who were in for the sort of crimes that Ryan was accused of were made targets among the outlaw population. Mercilessly harassed and mortally threatened by the other inmates in the Yuma jail, Ryan was quickly separated from the rest of the prisoners for his own safety. But in reality there was no safe place for John Ryan, because when all was said and done, he was his own worst enemy.

The three years that Ryan occupied cell 14 could hardly have been called tranquil. Perpetually pacing through the darkness of his cell, Ryan was always awake, often spending his evening hours roaring every profanity a man can utter into the darkness. More than once, his rants resulted in his banishment into the "Dark Cell," where he suffered solitary confinement in complete darkness for days at a time. By March 31, 1903, Ryan's unknown demons finally got the better of him. He was found in cell 14, hanging by the neck from a rope he made with the blankets in his room.

Yet this wasn't the last the world would hear of John Ryan. Throughout the years, the strange sights and sounds plaguing cell 14 have repeatedly brought the name of the tortured frontiersman to the lips of the living. It is largely believed that Ryan's ghost is largely responsible for the strange occurrences there. Though the Yuma Territorial Prison was shut down on September 15, 1909, roughly six years after Ryan passed away, it has never really been completely abandoned. Throughout the 1920s and 1930s, the prison was used as a shelter by hobos and the homeless; during the following years, locals took to cannibalizing parts of the compound for building materials.

In the more recent past, the former prison has become something of a tourist attraction. Registered as a state historic park, the old prison complex has become a destination for all sorts of people over the years. It is the experiences of these visitors in and around cell 14 that have turned John Ryan from another sad story of the Old West to one of the region's most popular ghosts.

People walking by cell 14 have heard the shuffling sounds coming from within the darkness of the barred room. Many of those who stop to take a closer look see nothing in the cell, the sound of someone's manic pacing suddenly replaced by silence. While this has caused more than one visitor to doubt his senses, others stopping before cell 14 have been subjected to sights, sounds and sensations strange enough to impel them to doubt their own sanity. These are the people who have looked upon the ghost of John Ryan.

Run-ins with this apparition are usually described in the same fashion. Witnesses feel an abrupt drop of temperature as they peer into the cell, and then—sometimes gradually, sometimes suddenly—he appears out of thin air. He appears in the back of the cell, a shadowy silhouette pacing across the width of the room, his only recognizable feature being two white lights shining faintly where his eyes should be. There one moment, gone the next, the ghost of John Ryan is never visible for more than a few seconds before vanishing from sight completely, leaving cell 14 unoccupied, empty as it was mere moments before.

Jesse Torres, an employee at the Yuma Territorial Prison State Historic Park, considers himself a skeptical man, not prone to buying into fantastical stories of the ghosts of tortured convicts. Nonetheless, he admits that there is something strange about cell 14. "There've been times when I've walked by the cells and gotten this eerie feeling. It's like, the temperature drops and something feels not quite right. I don't know if I believe in ghosts, but this has happened to me more than once." Rationalizing the experience, Jesse says that the experience may well be a figment of his imagination, but even as the words come out of his mouth, he sounds slightly uncertain. He concludes his account of cell 14 by falling back on historical fact, concrete information he can rely on. "Whatever the case, John Ryan was an all-around badman, so bad that none of the other inmates wanted anything to do with him."

Has the inborn evil that tortured Ryan while he was alive remained in cell 14? Is this what some witnesses are seeing when they peer through the iron bars? Is this what Jesse Torres feels when he walks by the long-abandoned room? Or is Ryan's ghost a paranormal expression of his earthly agony, a sort of psychic imprint left behind in the same cell he spent the last years of his life in? Whatever the case, John Ryan, who lived most of his life in bitter anonymity, could never have guessed that people would be talking about him in the 21st century. Given the conditions of his tragic story, it would probably be best if we had nothing to talk about, but as long as the apparition continues to haunt cell 14 in the Yuma Territorial Prison, this poor outlaw's morbid tale will not be allowed to rest.

6
Working
Men

The Legend of the Lost Lemon Mine

Thoughts of fire and gold possessed Lafayette French as he lay on his deathbed. Fire because his entire body was covered in burns, and every movement he made, from breathing to blinking, sent the searing memory of flame coursing through his bones. Gold because he had organized an expedition for the lost Lemon Mine only two days before and would have been on the back of a horse riding north at that instant if his cabin hadn't caught fire and come down on him in a burning heap on the very morning he was to begin his journey. The fact that he would never claim the untold riches of the rumored gold vein tortured French as much as the flame that had crippled him.

Not only crippled—Lafayette French knew that he dying. He was covered in ointment and wrapped in bandages from head to toe. The old man's breath came in rattling gasps; his limbs were immobile, paralyzed by the fire that continued to burn beneath his mangled skin. Unable even to speak, he only stared above at the wooden beams of the frontier cabin he was interred within, listening to the Montana wind howl outside as he obsessed over the details of his own demise. French was loathe to admit it, but as each anguished breath brought him closer to his end, he came to accept that the curse of the Lemon Mine had taken another man.

It was early in the month of July 1884 when French penned his last words to a friend in Helena:

Jeb,

The words you are reading here are likely to be my last. Things have gone badly wrong since last time I wrote. The expedition I was putting together for Frank Lemon's Mine last month never amounted to spit. There was a fire the night before we were to leave, and I've been badly hurt. I'm in bad, Jeb. Nobody's saying anything to me, but I'm sure I'll be buried within a week. Truthfully, I'll be glad to go, this is the kind of hurt that a man ain't meant to live through. As for the mine, I rue the day I listened to Frank Lemon, and should have never went after the gold that has taken too many men to an early grave. I'd tell you where it is Jeb, but I don't want to die thinking that I've sent you to your doom. The mine is damned, and any-one who goes after its gold is damned as well.

Be happy to have your health,
Lafayette

As he predicted, Lafayette French died three days after he sent the letter. Jeb took his friend's last words to heart, leaving the pursuit of the Lemon Mine to other, more foolhardy, fortune seekers.

These seekers were in no short supply in the years following French's death. It was the 1880s, and the West was teeming with men who were willing to bet their lives for a stab at riches. And so they came, footing it up every rocky slope in the Alberta Rockies from Waterton River to the Bow, hoping to find that glorious mother lode discovered by a man called Blackjack and his cohort, Frank Lemon, in 1871. The brutal account of the founding pair's expedition was only the first chapter of the bizarre and tragic story of the mine, a tale that would continue for as long as there were men who sought its treasure. While not all men who went after the mine ended up dead, it was said that the closer men got, the more likely tragedy would befall them. Throughout the rest of the 19th century, many more prospectors met an untimely death searching for the Lemon Mine in the upper reaches of the Kananaskis.

Of all the hopefuls who went up looking for the gold, only the first, Frank Lemon, had set eyes on the vein and lived to tell about it, though the experience ultimately cost him his sanity. His story begins in 1870, when a young Lafayette French—the same man who would burn to death 14 years later—commissioned Frank Lemon, a man called Blackjack and 30 others to investigate rumors of gold in the South Saskatchewan River. The group set out from the Tobacco Plains in the northwest corner of Montana during the springtime of that year. It would be a long, hard and dismally uneventful trip. For most of them.

Lemon and Blackjack would never have discovered the gold if it weren't for Blackjack's amazing ability to sniff out the shining metal from miles away. According to legend, this mysterious prospector was one of the first to discover gold in British Columbia's Cariboo, inaugurating the historic gold rush in that region. He made several famous gold strikes during the early days of the Cariboo rush, and many of his gold-digging peers soon believed that he had some sort of sixth sense when it came to the whereabouts of the precious metal.

A prospector with his supplies outside his tent in 1884

So it was that Frank Lemon took it seriously when Blackjack woke him early one morning before the sun had risen, whispering that he had a hard hunch about a gold vein in the surrounding mountains. "There's gold in these hills,"

Blackjack said to the instantly alert Lemon, "and I don't feel the need to share it with any of these fools."

Lemon looked from the snoring men sprawled throughout the camp, to Blackjack, who was crouched before him. In the starlight, he could make out a broad smile on the eager man's face. Lemon thought about it for all of a second before nodding his head. "Count me in."

The pair packed what supplies they needed while the rest of the men in the expedition were still asleep and quickly stole away, beginning their ascent up the side of the nearest mountain. Blackjack's gut feeling was as reliable as it ever was. When the two came across a roaring alpine stream, he offhandedly suggested that they hike up to its headwaters. It was hard going to the top; the path they made over the mountain was dense forest and sheer rock. They clambered over avalanche paths, cut their way through thick bush and climbed the sides of cliffs. By the time they reached the source of the anonymous creek, both men were scraped up, sweaty and beyond exhaustion.

Indeed, if it weren't for the sight that greeted them at the top, it is doubtful that Blackjack and Lemon would've been able to stay on their feet. But as it stood, the light shining from the ledge of gold jutting out of the rock was a salve to their pain. Before them was more mineral wealth than either man could ever have dreamed to see in his life. It took a few minutes before the realization sunk in. And when it did, their whoops of joy echoed over the mountaintops. They were rich.

"By Lucifer and all his fallen angels!" Lemon yelled into the sky, "Look what we found. It's pure goddamn gold! And it's all ours, Blackjack!" Lemon threw his arms around his partner, tears of happiness streaming down his dirty face. Blackjack only grinned as he looked at the glittering mother lode, thinking that maybe now he could put his gold-digging days behind him. There was enough gold here to make a dozen paupers into princes.

But in the end, neither Lemon nor Blackjack took a single nugget. Something happened as the sun began to sink under the jagged horizon—something deep and dark and ugly. With the deepening shadows of dusk came suspicion and doubt. The two prospectors, huddled around their fire, got lost in the darkness of their own thoughts as a hard wind came to life atop the mountain. Eerie and unnatural sounds came on the fitful gusts. Rocks rolling down the mountain echoed in frightful reverberations as bizarre howls and grunts came from distances near and far.

There are many different versions of exactly what transpired on the mountain that night, but every account has Frank Lemon succumbing to evil. They began to fight over their plans for the gold mine. Lemon, suddenly convinced that Blackjack was trying to swindle him, thought that the two should start digging out the ore at day break. Blackjack disagreed, saying that they would do much better if they headed back to Montana and got an investor to back a large excavation. The argument quickly got out of hand, and the two men would've surely come to blows if Blackjack hadn't gotten a grip on himself. "Wait one second here, hombre!" the veteran prospector roared at his angry confederate. "What kind of madness is this? Why don't we just calm down? We'll have all sorts of time to talk when this dastardly night is over." With that, Blackjack tucked himself into his bedroll, put his back to a cowed Lemon and went to sleep.

If Blackjack believed that he had gotten through to Lemon, he was sorely mistaken. According to some versions of the story, Lemon became possessed by voices in the darkness—diabolical whispers that told him to commit murder. Other accounts have Lemon being motivated by a lethal combination of greed and paranoia. Either way, the outcome was the same. Frank Lemon waited until Blackjack had fallen asleep before he crawled out of bed, picked up his ax and drove it into the sleeping prospector's skull.

An instant later, the evil that had been, until then, whispering on the wind broke out into a full-blown roar. The wind picked up to a blustering howl the moment the ax came down, and a hideous cackle sounded over the peak, as if some evil being in the darkness took great joy at what had just happened. All thoughts of the gold vein vanished on the spot as Lemon fell to the ground, blubbering scared at the evil he had woken. He threw fuel on the campfire, hoping to drive away whatever was lurking just beyond the light. All his efforts got him was a clearer look at what was there. He saw it staring at him from beyond the dead body of Blackjack, standing over the gold vein that had driven him to murder: an enormous black figure with two burning red eyes glaring at him in fiendish glee. Whatever sanity Frank Lemon could call his own went up in smoke then and there. Without another thought, the frantic man turned his back on the gold and ran as fast as his boots could take him.

Miraculously, Lemon survived his headlong dash down the rocky slope that night. He was spotted by fur trappers a few days later, a drooling, babbling mess, repeating the same words over and over again: "There's a devil on the mountain." Making it back to the Tobacco Plains just before winter set in, Lemon was no longer recognizable to the friends who had known him before he left. Lafayette French was especially shocked at the shape Lemon was in. Concerned about the fate of his expedition north, French tried to get Lemon's story out of him, but the afflicted man was far too incoherent to relate his story to anyone. The only evidence he had of the rich vein they had discovered were two fist-sized nuggets of gold that he had stashed in his pockets.

Wherever he looked, Lemon saw Blackjack's face in horrifying clarity—a rotting head appearing in every shadow, leering at its killer with morbid joy. The weeks passed, and Lemon's condition worsened. Unable to come to terms with what he had done, Lemon was consumed by guilt, and it wasn't long before the distraught man was looking for a sympathetic ear. He found that in Lafayette French, who hadn't stopped prying for details about the expedition he had financed. Dying to unburden his conscience, Lemon told French everything in one feverish confession—his and Blackjack's desertion, their hike up the mountain, their gilded discovery, Blackjack's murder and the dark, horrifying creature with the two red eyes.

As incredible as Lemon's story was, French had stopped listening the moment Lemon mentioned the gold. Blackjack's death didn't concern him in the least, and the hardened frontiersman wasn't at all scared of some red-eyed creature on a mountaintop. Frank Lemon was sobbing like a child after he finished his tale, but all Lafayette could think about was the gold. "Straighten up there, Frank," Lafayette told the weeping man, "you can't be blamed for the death of a man you couldn't trust. Wasn't it his idea to ditch the crew and head up the mountain?" Lafayette put a consoling hand on Frank's back. "If he told everyone about his secret stash, this thing would've never happened."

"You reckon?" Frank replied hopefully, looking at Lafayette French.

"Sure I do. I know what your problem is. Ol' Blackjack never got a proper burial, and your good God-lovin' soul isn't letting you rest over it. Why don't you tell me where the man lies, and I'll get someone to go on up there and bury that man proper."

That was all it took to get the distressed man to tell everything he knew, so eager was he at any chance to rid himself of his visions. For his part, French was true to his word, paying an experienced half-breed named John McDougall to go to the mountain and bury Blackjack. McDougall returned the following spring, announcing that he had found the mine and buried Blackjack's body. He also told French that Lemon's description of the gold vein wasn't an exaggeration; he had seen the mother lode on the mountaintop, and it was every bit as big as Lemon said it was.

The second expedition to the mine took place soon after McDougall's return. That spring, Frank Lemon seemed to be cured of the demon that haunted him, and he eagerly took French up on his offer to lead a group of 10 men to the gold. It would be the first of many fruitless hunts for the cursed lode. What looked to have been a sure thing on the Montana border fell apart with every step the gold diggers took towards the Kananaskis Valley.

The first indication that Frank Lemon's recovery wasn't all it was cracked up to be came within the first week. Horrible apparitions came to visit Lemon in the night. Each night, the men would be woken by their leader's manic screams. They started as nightmarish visions that came and went in minutes, but before long Frank was running through camp, waving his ax at whatever invisible attackers were coming at him. Lemon got worse and worse the closer they got to the gold vein. By the time they crossed the Bow River, he was strung up on the back of his horse, begging hysterically to be let go, roaring at the top of his lungs that if they didn't turn around, certain death was waiting at the end of the trail. Spooked by Lemon's descent into madness and sure they would never find the mine without Frank's help, the outfit abandoned their mission just before they reached the Kananaskis Valley. If the men were disappointed at the outcome of their aborted expedition, the affair made Frank into a complete wreck. He would spend the rest of his days an invalid in his uncle's ranch in Texas, where he never left his room but only stared out the window of his second-story room, looking silently at the northern horizon.

Frank's fate left a mark on the people of the Tobacco Plains, and everyone who heard the story took to calling the gold vein in the Canadian Rockies the Lemon Mine. And so was born the legend of the Lemon Mine—a tragic tale that grew with each mishap and mortality suffered by those who went after it. There would be many.

Lafayette French paid his trusty friend John McDougall to go back to the mine after Lemon's failed attempt, but McDougall would never make it there. Indeed, he never even made it out of Montana. A few days after he departed, McDougall was seen wandering into a Fort Kipp saloon. Looking haggard and haunted, the frontiersman ordered one drink after another without saying a word to anyone. An avowed teetotaler, McDougall had never touched a drop of liquor in his entire life. No one knows what pulled him to the bottle during the first leg of his journey, but it must have been bad, because McDougall ended up drinking himself to death in that Fort Kipp saloon.

Though people had begun speaking of a curse over the Lemon Mine after McDougall died, French was still undeterred. He put together an expedition that he planned to lead himself, but as it turned out, he never even got a chance to walk out his front door. A fire roared through French's cabin the night before he was going to head out. Badly burned, French died of his wounds a few days later, the exact location of the lode following French to his grave.

In the following years, the Lost Lemon Mine became something of a Holy Grail among western American gold diggers, a priceless treasure that, as it turned out, would never be found. Or was it? Countless miners went up into the Kananaskis; a good number of them were never seen again. Did those who laid eyes on the Lemon Mine end up succumbing to its curse? While no one can say for sure, the Stony Indians indigenous to the Kananaskis region have long regarded the lost alpine riches ensconced atop one of their mountains to be evil. Indeed, several folklorists have speculated that a long-dead Stony chief, dismayed at the flood of white men that followed any gold strike, put a curse on the gold to keep prospectors away. If this is the case, it worked, because no one has ever found the Lost Lemon Mine, and to this day, Kananaskis Country stands as one of the best preserved wilderness parks on the continent.

The Mamie R. Mine

Compared to the feverish enthusiasm of most gold rushes in the American West, the gold mining in Colorado's Cripple Creek region had surprisingly tentative, if not downright skeptical, origins. Located in central Colorado, 25 miles west of Pike's Peak, the Cripple Creek area was a quiet place, used mostly for grazing livestock by local homesteaders. One would think that Bob Womack's discovery of gold in 1874 would have made the quiet creek into another one of the West's gold-digging Gomorrahs, but no such thing happened…well, not *yet* anyway. Spurred on by his modest 1874 finding, Womack put his back into the job. He must have been imbued with an amazing stubbornness.

Sixteen years passed before he made another strike—16 years of working alone, obstinately boring into the ground while the other gold diggers rushed from one bonanza to another. He was unmoved when they announced that there was gold in the Black Hills in 1876; he barely even looked up when word got out that men were making millions digging silver in Leadville in 1878. Yet even when Womack made his second discovery in 1890, it can't be said that it paid off.

Yes, other men finally took notice when Womack wandered into Denver with saddlebags full of gold ore. And yes, the first prospectors began to trickle into Cripple Creek soon after, a small number of hopefuls willing to make a gamble. It could be called the first stage of the Cripple Creek gold rush—not that any of this would make a difference to Womack. Spending the next year digging for gold alongside the newly arrived prospectors, Womack's labors were just as fruitless as they had been for most of the previous 16 years.

Many miners would die in the Cripple Creek mines. The Mamie R. tunnel was the most infamous for the strange whispers heard in its depths.

Indeed, 1891 was a hard year for all the prospectors at Cripple Creek, so hard that the site was abandoned by all but the most stubborn. Womack himself finally decided he had his fill of Cripple Creek; he sold his claim to a man named John P. Grannis for a mere $300. Womack would regret that sale for the rest of his life.

Later on that year, two men remembered only as Pat and Mike decided to try one more dig before they abandoned

Cripple Creek. As a lark, the two men agreed that they would dig on the next spot that their dog stopped to relieve itself. It turned out that the dog's nose for gold was superior to theirs. Digging into the hard ground where their dog had just defecated, the pair promptly hit an enormous gold vein. Three weeks later, Pat and Mike dug out $100,000 in ore. The rush was on.

What Womack had sold for $300 was suddenly worth over a hundred times that. Overnight, Cripple Creek real estate became the hottest property in the United States as prospectors from every corner of the continent flooded into the region. Dance halls, gambling halls, hotels, saloons, parlor houses and flophouses—Cripple Creek seemed to spring from the very rock. By the end of 1892, over 10,000 people were living in Cripple Creek. The mining operations would last an incredibly long time by gold rush standards, with the last serious Cripple Creek Mine closing down in 1961. Miners would dig up over 21 million ounces of gold from the Colorado earth in the nearly 70 years Cripple Creek mines were active.

Today, scores of abandoned mines are littered throughout the Cripple Creek region, ghostly husks of expired industry that mark the location of subterranean tunnels long since gutted of any gold they once contained. If these old head-frames could talk, theirs would be tales of hardship, desperation and avarice—of tough men burrowing beneath the earth for mineral wealth, emerging from tunnels battered, bruised and beyond exhaustion, lucky, in the end, if they emerged at all. Indeed, far too many of these men would meet gruesome deaths while toiling under western ground. The Cripple Creek mines would kill many a gold digger before they were closed for good. And of all the lethal tunnels that were dug around Cripple Creek, the Mamie R. on Raven Hill became the most infamous.

Men who worked the Mamie R. knew there was something wrong from the very beginning. Early diggers would talk of the strange voices they heard in the depths. They spoke of voices that seemed to come from the very rock, coming at them from the damp darkness, sometimes low and guttural, other times high and tittering. Many tried to disregard the mysterious voices, explaining them away as echoes from other men in nearby tunnels. But some miners offered up far more disturbing explanations. Some of the men who worked the Mamie R. were mining veterans, men who had worked the coal seams in Cornwall and the pits of Cape Breton—men who were well acquainted with the denizens of the deep.

These were the miners who grew increasingly uneasy at the sounds in the Mamie R.'s tunnels. In hushed whispers they talked about the deathly creatures that wreaked so much havoc in other mines. "It's them knackers," they would say. "Creatures or spirits, no man can say for sure, but they live underground, hidden from the sun, and they've sent far too many good men to graves they didn't deserve. Make no mistake, there's evil in this mine."

Nevertheless, gold fever held the Mamie R. workers in such a thrall that few were all that worried about whispers in the dark. Until, that is, the accidents began to occur. The first tragedy happened in the early evening, when five men breaking gold ore off one of the tunnel walls were suddenly interrupted by one of their coworkers, a Texan by the name of Hank Bull. "Hold up for one second," the grimy miner called out to the others. "I swore I heard something down there."

Miners took to calling the ghostly creatures in the Mamie R. "Tommy-knockers." They were known for their viciousness.

Through the dim light of the hanging lanterns, the miners could see Hank's massive form standing very still in the tunnel. He was staring intently down the shaft. "What you hear down there, Hank?" one of the men asked.

"I heard someone callin' my name."

"Down there?" another miner snorted, "man, you been chewin' peyote? There ain't nothin' down there but more of this blasted rock. Now let's get back to work."

One of the men raised his pickax and was just about to let it fall when Hank stopped him. "Don't!" Hank snapped at the man with the raised pickax. "You guys must have heard *that*."

"Heard what?"

"That!" Hank said again, his head snapping towards some noise that none of the others could hear.

"What are you talkin' about, fool?"

"There's a boy down there, a little boy. He's calling out for me. You guys can't be telling me you don't hear him."

The conviction in Hank's voice was such that each of the miners stopped and listened carefully, their heads bent toward the tunnel. Long moments passed, but no one heard a sound from the shaft below, nothing but water dripping into gathering puddles and the occasional pebble rolling down the tunnel wall. "Nothin' there, Hank," one of the miners finally said. "Besides, how could there be? That stretch was just dug yesterday. No one would be foolish enough to go down there 'til the shaft is braced."

Hank was unmoved. "I'm going to take a gander for a second. I'll be back."

One of his coworkers called out to him, warning him that the tunnel ahead wasn't safe, that it hadn't been braced yet, but Hank gave no sign he heard as he disappeared down the tunnel. The miners all got quiet, listening to the sound of Hank Bull's boots fall on loose rock. Then there was nothing—not a sound. One minute passed, two minutes passed, and the miners were still as statues in the absolute silence of the shaft, trying their best to fight a rising tide of fear. It seemed as if the water had stopped dripping, even the miners' labored breathing rose and fell without a sound. And then, with a suddenness that sent each of the men into spasms of terror, the silence was broken by a horrifying scream. It was Hank, his voice so fearful that it was almost unrecognizable.

Half the men jumped back to the tunnel entrance, the other half leapt forward to help their distressed coworker, but none of them made it too far before the tunnel ahead caved in. The miners looked on helplessly as the unsupported ceiling above Hank came down, burying the hapless miner under a pile of rubble. Mamie R. workers on the surface felt the earth rumble as rock dust billowed from the mine entrance. The bucket was promptly lowered into the mine, and one by one, each of the men was brought out of the tunnels alive…except for Hank Bull. The poor man was long dead when the workers finally pulled his remains out of the tunnel. His body, smashed and badly mangled, was almost unrecognizable, but it was his face, twisted into an expression of the most profound terror, that left the greatest impression on the men who dug him out.

In daylight hours, very little was said about Hank's last moments in the mine—the voice he claimed to hear, his bloodcurdling scream just before the tunnel collapsed. Yet the story of his demise circulated in whiskey-soaked conversations and short whispers. All the while, the mysterious whispers and moving shadows continued within the depths of the Mamie R., and it wasn't long before the miners began deserting the Mamie R.

They left in droves, and soon only a skeleton crew remained to mine the depths of the Mamie R. Bold, stupid or just extraordinarily avaricious, these stubborn men stayed on even as the bizarre goings-on at the bottom of the mine got weirder. They dug deeper and deeper under Raven Hill, all the while ignoring the growing strangeness that no one could explain.

Barely audible whispers in the dark turned into distinct voices, though no one could say what strange and guttural language these voices were speaking. Some claimed to see dark figures moving in their peripheral vision, figures that would vanish into the walls whenever the miners turned to get a better look. Not knowing what they were dealing with, the miners of the Mamie R. took to calling the beings in the dark "Tommyknockers" and tried did their best to work alongside them. The Tommyknockers, however, were not nearly so cooperative.

They seemed to take a special interest to the windlass system that transported men and ore from the tunnels to the surface. Men below would ring a signal bell three times to be hauled up above ground in the windlass bucket. Yet on too many occasions, the bell would be rung, the bucket would be hauled up and nothing, neither men nor ore, would be there. If the miners were puzzled by this the first few times it occurred, they quickly grew accustomed to the skullduggery. "Damn Tommyknockers," miners would grumble, "don't they have any respect for a man trying to earn his living?"

Before long, miners of the Mamie R. discovered that the Tommyknockers' malice ran much deeper than mere disrespect. The second death in the mine occurred in late November 1894, when a miner standing at the bottom of the entrance shaft had his skull crushed by the windlass bucket, which had come loose of the cable and plummeted down the pit. While all in the Mamie R. mourned the death of another miner, no one could explain how the bucket had come loose; the windlass rope was still intact and the knot that was tied to the bucket was still fastened tight. Given the evidence, there was no way the bucket could have come loose. If any of the men working the mine had gotten used to the Tommyknockers, the incident hardened their suspicion of those mysterious creatures in the mine.

In turn, the strange happenings in the mine increased dramatically. Some miners claimed that they could hear the Tommyknockers closer than ever, as if they were standing right next to them, whispering unintelligible threats into their ears. Anyone turning to get a look at these creatures would find nothing there but the damp darkness of the Mamie R. It did not stop there. At the end of the workday, many exhausted miners claimed to catch glimpses of small horned creatures, standing no more than 3 feet off the ground, dashing about in obvious glee, leaping to and fro in some sort of demented dance, celebrating the miners' departure. It was always dark when the miners caught sight of these creatures, and while no one claimed to seem them clearly, those who did always offered the same description: short, with two horns jutting out of their heads, and burning red eyes.

Whether the Tommyknockers were getting bolder as the miners dug deeper or had simply grown tired of the miners' presence might not ever be known, but in the weeks after the second miner's death, the feeling in the Mamie R. became almost intolerable. In addition to the now near-constant hiss of angry voices and darting shadows, some miners claimed to see the apparitions of their recently departed coworkers. A badly injured Hank Bull was seen in the deepest recesses of the mine, walking through the tunnels with a completely expressionless look on his bleeding face. Men hoisting the windlass bucket out of the mine at the sound of the signal bell would stand back in terror as the apparition of the second dead miner would silently emerge from the well, his blank eyes staring listlessly from his crushed skull. Moving to get out of the bucket, the wounded apparition would vanish the moment its foot touched the surface.

And still, the men of the Mamie R. remained resolute, digging their ore out from the tunnel walls without complaint. Until, that is, Christmas Day 1894, a few weeks after the second miner was killed, when another miner was killed in a freakish accident. The circumstances of this death were so improbable, and so absolutely gruesome, that each and every man in the Mamie R. abandoned the mine, never to return.

The Mamie R. had flooded on Christmas Eve, and the miners had spent most of the next day hauling water out of the tunnels, one bucket at a time. Three men worked the windlass on the surface, hoisting buckets of water out of the well as they were filled. It happened in an instant. The windlass, groaning under the weight of the buckets of water, suddenly came apart: the winding spool that the rope was wrapped around flew off the frame, causing a dozen yards of rope to come loose as the bucket full of water plummeted down the shaft. One of the men on the surface had become entangled in the slack rope, which was quickly snaking down the well along with the bucket. The line hit the end of the loose cord, snapping taut and cleanly decapitating the man who has been draped in the rope. Apparently a coil had settled on his shoulders, and when the rope was pulled tight by the force of the falling bucket, it sliced through his neck like a razor-sharp knife. No one tried to explain how the winding spool had come off the windlass. The miners had had enough; convinced that the Tommyknockers were responsible for the three fatal accidents in the mine, every one of the miners quit that Christmas. Word of the cursed Mamie R. spread throughout Cripple Creek, and no one from the mining community would replace the workers. By late January 1895, the mine atop Raven Hill was officially closed—its depths never plumbed for gold again.

While the story of the Mamie R. mine has become a legend in the ghostlore of the West, Colorado's State Bureau of Mines has no record that it ever existed. Skeptics have used this fact to debunk the story of the Mamie R. If every other mine that was dug in the Cripple Creek region is listed, why not the alleged Mamie R.? The response has come with the argument that the Mamie R. operated only until 1894, and the bureau's census of Cripple Creek began one year later, in 1895. Being one of the few mines that closed before the bureau took its census, it was never included in the bureau's books, and thus was lost in the historical record.

And so it is—as it is with many such legends—that belief depends more upon gut feeling and faith than any immutable proof. Were the Tommyknockers in the Mamie R. one and the same as the "Knackers" of Cornish legend, alive and well under American earth? If so, what, exactly, were they? Subterranean beasts with a fierce dislike for humanity? Or perhaps evil or disconsolate spirits awoken by miners' pickaxes and dynamite? No one knows for sure. Some have guessed that the Mamie R. might have been situated on an Indian burial ground, and the Tommyknockers were Indian spirits angered at having their rest disturbed on account of gold diggers' greed. Others have likened the Tommyknockers to goblins and kobolds, mythic European creatures that have a natural hatred for humans. Whatever the case, if the Tommyknockers do indeed exist under Cripple Creek, and if they are as vicious as the legend of the Mamie R. would have us believe, it is probably a case of the less we know, the better.

The Angry Ghost of Jack Myers

Jack Myers was about as bad as they came. A man who swilled booze, stole and murdered with equal zeal, he cut his teeth riding with a band of outlaws in the Wyoming Territory during the late 1880s. His exceptional brutality and skill with his six-shooter quickly elevated him above his dissolute gang. While the others in his retinue were content in sticking to armed robbery and the occasional beating, Myers relished the more lethal aspects of his dubious trade and killed more than one man just to see the look on his victim's face. He was said to have cut down four men in Wyoming before the law chased him out.

From there, Meyers made his way up to the logging frontier in the northwest, where he made the rough town of Port Blackely, Washington, his new center of operations. As in Wyoming, Myers' "operations" involved practically every kind of crime a person can imagine. Living now amongst loggers, Myers gambled, drank, robbed and fought, responsible for more than his fair share of devilry in Port Blackely. The first time he was thrown in the calaboose it was for stealing lumber; the second time, it was for forgery. Myers served only a few months of his second sentence when he

While cramped living quarters and fights were common in logging camps, an atmosphere of dread made Taylor Logging Camp infamous.

escaped from jail, making his way north up the coast to Canada's Gulf Islands.

Things changed for the itinerant outlaw when he crossed the border. Trading in his horse for an 18-foot sloop, Myers took his banditry to the Strait of Georgia, hopping from island to island, selling bootlegged whiskey to thirsty loggers. It may have been a far cry from the hills of Wyoming, but Myers managed to make it work. While his illegal operation satisfied the inbred rule-breaker in him, the rough logging camps suited his coarse disposition just fine.

The camps were hard places, full of single young men who worked beyond exhaustion every day, felling the enormous evergreens along the coast for a pittance. When it was time to unwind, the loggers turned their humble settlements into pockets of roaring revelry, complete with every sort of vice that could be found in any cattle town on the range or mining camp in the mountains. Myers was there to provide the fuel for these shindigs, arriving in his one-man ship with barrels full of stolen booze.

The small, sinewy outlaw was doing a fine business until his island-hopping enterprise brought him to the shores of Read Island. A lush islet covered in a rich layer of old-growth forest, Read Island became a logging center in the early 1890s when Americans and Europeans began flooding into the region, looking to turn the forest into funds. It was a chaotic process, and nothing demonstrated this better than the goings-on at the island's infamous Taylor Logging Camp.

According to some, there was something on the island that defied ready classification—a vague uneasiness that was barely palpable in the thick coastal forest, that hovered just beyond vision over the surrounding waters. More than an impression but less than a feeling, it was described as an indefinite sense of distant dread, as if something with evil intentions was approaching from a great distance. The sense was that while there was still time, it was running out. No reason was ever provided to explain this sense, but some believed that the island was haunted. It was said that the southern tip of the island was the site of a horrible massacre, where a village of Indians had been attacked and destroyed by a Kwakliuth war party. Some believed that the ghosts of this massacre were responsible for the strange energy that could be felt throughout the island.

Such an energy might explain the nature of Taylor Logging Camp. For while such settlements were never the gentlest places, this Read Island camp was possessed by an especially vicious sort of culture. It seemed as if every man there was running with a short fuse. Distracted, irritable and all too eager to get soused, the men of Taylor were more than capable of bringing hell to the Strait of Georgia.

Myers certainly felt it when he beached his vessel on Read Island. Quickly getting in touch with the camp's distributor, Myers sold his stolen rotgut, and then, as was his custom, settled down to enjoy what mayhem the place could provide. He wouldn't be disappointed in Taylor. Getting thoroughly trashed the first night he was there, Myers was impressed by the level of lunacy in the camp. The loggers drank too much, gambled too much and talked too much, a combination of traits that resulted in several bloody brawls before the night was up.

Myers was more than willing to get into the spirit of things, and on the second night he was there, he found himself throwing back shot after shot of his own whiskey and getting on as many men's nerves as he could manage. But it wasn't until a man got on *his* nerves that things took a turn for the worse. He had lost a big bet in a hand of poker to one of the camp's loggers. The loss itself was bad enough, but the excessive delight of the man who had won his money was even worse. A young logger who had just taken more money than he probably saw in half a year, he whooped and hollered over the din of the drinking tent, milking his win for everything he could.

"Whoa there," Myers grumbled at the exultant young man, "it ain't the Fourth of July, boy. Settle down."

"Who you callin' boy?" came the response. "Ain't no whelp in this room but the man who just lost all his money. Now get out of my sight, moonshiner."

Such conversation was run-of-the-mill in Taylor, but Myers wasn't a run-of-the-mill man. He had killed for less than this when he had been in a better mood. "Say that again, boy?" the trashed degenerate said, his hand falling to the handle of his six-shooter. His opponent was unarmed, but the look in Myers' eye made it clear that he didn't care. The tent went quiet. "I said, say that again, you worthless piece of dirt. I dare you to say that again."

The logger knew then that he had bitten off more than he could chew. His glance went from the shooting iron strapped to Myers' hip to the homicidal glint in the man's eye. He was scared, and suddenly very sober, but still couldn't lose face in front of his coworkers. He gave his best attempt at a cocky grin. "C'mon now, man, I was just horsin' around."

"Well I ain't," Myers replied. "Now I want you to repeat what it was that you said. I gotta be sure I heard right before I shoot you down."

That was when Jack O'Conner stepped forward. O'Conner was something of an anomaly on Read Island. A quiet, gentle logger, O'Conner was a giant of a man who didn't get involved in the licentious culture of the logging camp. He never drank; he never gambled; O'Conner just kept his head down and did his work. Indeed, until this very moment, most men in the camp hadn't even heard him speak.

"Now slow down here," O'Conner said to Myers, his voice slow and heavy. "The boy didn't mean any harm; let it go."

If these would have been reasonable words to most men, to Myers, they were a challenge; the ornery badman looked at O'Conner, noticed he was unarmed and decided to take him up on it. "Well lookit here," he slurred, "if it ain't Paul Bunyan himself." A moment passed where both men just stared at each other.

"Malarkey," O'Conner said.

"What're you gonna do about it?"

There would be no more words. Myers jumped to his feet and went for his gun as O'Conner lunged. The big man's open grasp was about an inch away from Myers when the gun roared. A slug tore through O'Conner's chest as he collapsed atop Myers, his hands wrapped around his adversary's throat. Still alive, O'Conner tightened his grip on Myers' neck and would have taken his killer with him if Myers didn't empty four more chambers into the lumberjack.

Pushing himself out from under a dead Jack O'Conner, Myers wasn't out of the tent when several loggers tackled him. To the credit of the men of Taylor, Jack Myers wasn't lynched on the spot, but disarmed, bound and held. Tried in November 1893, Myers was found guilty of manslaughter and sentenced to life in prison in the provincial penitentiary. He wouldn't make it one year into his sentence. Shot dead the next fall when he tried to make his escape from a prison-assigned work gang, the outlaw was buried like so many other men of his ilk: with next to no ceremony and even less emotion.

While this would be the end of the small man's dismal life, the story of this two-bit killer would continue to be told far longer than anyone could have anticipated. By all rights,

Myers should have been forgotten moments after he was laid underground, but that is without taking his posthumous activities into account. For not long after a prison guard's bullet found its mark in the back of Myers' head, strange things began being reported in Reading Island.

Not that strange things hadn't been reported at Read Island before. Loggers had long noted the inexplicable tension in the air on the island, the vaguely humanoid shapes that formed out of the morning mist drifting in off the water, the distant cries of terror that were often heard in the middle of the night that woke more than one lumberjack from fitful dreams. These phenomena had been talked about since the first day loggers began plying their trade on the wooded islet.

The occurrences that began after Jack Myers was killed, however, were far more vivid, and witnessed by many more people. It is not known who it was that saw him first, but according to legend, he appeared late in 1894. It was Jack Myers, or something that looked very much like the physically diminutive murderer. If the vision hadn't been faintly transparent, pale as bone and bleeding heavily from his head, the witness may have believed that Myers had escaped from prison. But there was no mistaking this apparition for anything on this side of the grav, and it filled all who saw it with an inexplicable wave of terror. Most men turned and ran at the sight of Myers. Those who managed to fight this instinct would be struck by an even more horrifying event, as the bleeding vision would lunge towards stunned onlookers, its face twisting into an expression of pure hatred. At this point, even the most solid hearted would turn and flee, not looking back until there was no more energy to run. Yet no exhausted glances over shoulders ever yielded another sighting; the angry ghost of Jack Myers was gone, leaving no trace that he had ever been there at all.

Over the years, he was spotted by countless lumberjacks all over the island. While his first appearances were limited to Taylor Logging Camp, it wasn't long before he was seen leering at loggers from within the shadows of trees and along mist-shrouded waters—there one moment, gone the next. If there were suspicions that Read Island was possessed by restless spirits prior to Jack Myers' arrival, they were confirmed after the outlaw was killed in prison. It seemed as if souls of the dead had a preternatural attraction to Read Island's wooded shores; certainly, Jack Myers felt comfortable there, and according to witnesses, he had lost none of his earthly viciousness.

Today, the southern tip of Read Island has been preserved as one of British Columbia's provincial parks. Campers, hikers, sightseers, kayakers and tourists all visit the island to enjoy its natural landscape; the island is a noted haven for bald eagles and also attracts birdwatchers to its rocky shores. As for the vague sense of foreboding so often talked about over a century ago, this seems to have all but vanished with the passage of years. Perhaps the arrival and departure of so many contented visitors have somehow crowded out the souls of past tragedy.

Nevertheless, some people have had experiences with a mysterious figure that seem reminiscent of the early loggers' tales. It is said that he appears in the woods, a short, impossibly pale man with a mustache and receding hairline, staring intently with no overabundance of kindness. While he has never done harm to anyone, no one who has seen him tarries in his company for too long. Witnesses have spoken of feeling a sudden coldness down their backs the moment they set eyes on the lone man, and though the figure doesn't move or make a sound, he manages to convey a sense of danger, as if he were a single whisper away from attack. Whether visitors back away slowly from him or turn and run, the encounters always end the same, with the man simply vanishing from sight.

And so it is that the legend of Jack Myers continues today, kept alive with every new sighting of the one-time six-gun marauder who made his way from the mountains of Wyoming to Canada's western islands. Why he chooses to remain behind on the island he visited for a few short days is anyone's guess, but at least his anger seems to have subsided, for there hasn't been a single report of Myers chasing down a man, woman or child. Or perhaps loggers are the ones that Myers hates, and he is only searching for another lumberjack, his angry ghost intent on chasing down those men he believes responsible for his incarceration and ultimate death. It is best, then, that the trees on the southern tip of Read Island have been allowed, once more, to grow.

THE END